THEATRE ROYAL
100 years of Stratford East

Theatre Royal

100 years of Stratford East

Michael Coren

Quartet Books

LONDON MELBOURNE NEW YORK

First published by Quartet Books Limited 1984
A member of the Namara Group
27/29 Goodge Street, London W1P 1FD

British Library Cataloguing in Publication Data

Coren, Michael
   Theatre royal 100 years of stratford east
   1. Theatre Royal (*Stratford*)—History
   I. Title
   792'.09421'76   PN2596.L7T5

ISBN 0-7043-2474-1

Typeset by MC Typeset, Chatham, Kent
Printed and bound in Great Britain
by Mackays of Chatham Ltd, Kent

To Robert Winder and Hermione Davies

Contents

Acknowledgements

More goodwill emanates from those who have worked at Stratford East over the years than is altogether decent. For that reason the number of people I should thank is very large, and not all of them are listed below. They will understand. Howard Goorney's *The Theatre Workshop Story* (Methuen) and Oscar Tapper's unpublished *The Other Stratford* were both useful. Two people whom I am for ever indebted are Jim Hiley, friend and mentor, and Philip Hedley, who gave me time and resources but never once tried to influence me in his favour. The following I heartily thank: Lindsay Anderson, Tony Banks, Clive Barker, Michael Billington, Howard Bloch, Mark Borkowski, Sara Drake, Nell Dunn, Mike Elphick, Bamber Gascoigne, Lord Gowrie, Nickolas Grace, Gary Grant, Steve Grant, Georgina Hale, Ken Hill, Maureen Lipman, Oscar Lowenstein, Tony Marchant, Murray Melvin, Warren Mitchell, Charles Morgan, Alan Plater, Peter Rankin, Joy Sapieka, Maxwell Shaw, Victor Spinetti, Maggi Taylor, Sue Timothy, Jack Tinker, Clare Venables, Maureen Vincent, Kate Williams and everybody I bothered during the writing of the book.

I am grateful for the companionship of John Hayes, Steve Hayhurst, Ava Kolouchova, John Pilger, Yvonne Roberts, Alex Sutherland, Tim Vass, Francis Wheen and Ian Willard. And a special note of thanks to my publisher, Naim Attallah, who has always been very encouraging.

Introduction

Whether a centenary should be commemorated or quietly ignored is open to question. But a hundredth birthday provides an opportunity both for sober reflection and for zealous story-telling. This book is intended to do both. There is, however, further justification for writing Stratford East's history: it has never been done before. And now that the theatre is threatened by closure the task is even more pressing.

One woman, whose name has been virtually synonymous with the history of Stratford East is Joan Littlewood. Her contribution to international theatre is immeasurable: Theatre Workshop changed the course of British drama. Since her departure a succession of actors and directors has laboured to keep the theatre alive, and their labours too are noteworthy.

Stratford East is much more than a theatre, and almost all who work there tell of an ambience which has to do with more than the lines of Shakespeare or the prose of a contemporary playwright. Walls, foundations, community all mingle together to produce what is now an old theatre with few financial resources in the middle of modern tower blocks and shopping centres, car parks and motorways.

Due to lack of written material I have relied heavily on a multitude of recorded interviews with people who have been involved with the theatre – cleaners, local enthusiasts, artistic directors – from the Second World War to the present. I did not manage to talk to Joan Littlewood. She did not answer my letters, and according to her close friends her reasons may be threefold: Stratford East is a shrine to her lover Gerry Raffles and thus should not be criticized; the theatre killed Raffles and should not be given the courtesy of being written about; and it has no story apart from Joan Littlewood's own.

Inevitably, my account will annoy and upset some. The theatre provokes partisan feelings, and those I've spoken to express their enthusiasms in no uncertain terms. That is the way Stratford has always been.

Michael Coren
Essex, July 1984

1.
Origins, Tears and Cheers

The phenomenon known as the 'pea-souper' was still very much a part of East End life during the last two decades of the nineteenth century. With its proximity to the river Thames and to the low lands of Essex, the outer London town of Stratford, often experienced mists which would have done justice to any low-budget film involving Jack the Ripper or Sherlock Holmes. The precise meteorological conditions in the area for Wednesday 17 December 1884 are not known; it is certain however, that although only days away from Christmas, there was no dense and impenetrable fog to mar the opening night of the Theatre Royal, Stratford East.

Elsewhere in the world that year the heroic but misguided General Gordon arrived at a besieged Khartoum to the cheers of all Europe; gold was discovered in a corner of Africa; and cocaine was used for the first time as an anaesthetic, with consequences ninety years later which would have horrified those good doctors. In Stratford the management and players of the Theatre Royal had been overworked and anxious since the announcement that the first night would be on 6 December. Their anxiety became near panic after a postponement of eleven days. The gentlemen of the press had been notified, handbills announcing the venue as 'two minutes walk from the Stratford Station, one from the Town Hall, and one from Maryland Point' posted, and price-lists announcing the cost of sixpence (2½p) for the gallery through to a place in the stalls for a shilling (5p) and a private box for a guinea (£1.5p) circulated.

The production was to be *Richelieu*, otherwise known as *The Conspiracy*, by the politician, historical novelist and prolific writer Lord Bulwer Lytton. It was a popular and popularly-known drama, so much so that some of the more staid members of the company were a little shocked at the unconventional audience, many of whom had already sampled the seasonal spirit. The important point was that local people had turned out in force to pass judgement on and show support for the new theatre.

Final preparations had been completed only directly prior to the opening, and complaints were made about the smell of fresh paint which still permeated the building. The odour may well have been caused by a new fire-proof solution which had been painted on the surface of every seat in the auditorium on the recommendation of the chief of the London Fire Brigade — the Captain Shaw made famous in Gilbert and Sullivan's *Iolanthe*.

The leading part of Cardinal Richelieu was to be played by the manager and founder of the theatre, Charles Dillon. Among his supporting actors were Archibald Graysdell, as the King, Frederick Thomas, playing the Chevalier de Mauprat, and Blanche Elliott, whose Julie de Mortemar was very well received by the critical audience. Most of the cast were well-known locally. As the curtain rose the theatre became silent, and then Charles Dillon appeared in his flowing red robes to a burst of applause. From all accounts the performance itself was usual for the period — more gesticulation than understanding — and although appreciated by most present there was some rowdiness. The *Era* for 20 December reported that:

Mr Dillon won much applause. He worked under difficulties and in one important scene had to interrupt the action of the play in order to reprove some inattentive gods who were appeasing their appetites. At the end of the act Mr Dillon very properly delivered the dwellers on high a lecture on the sin of cracking nuts, and it is to be hoped they will profit by his very earnest reproof. 'You treat me fairly,' said Mr Dillon, 'and I will treat you fairly, and give you good entertainment; but I will certainly not have the beautiful lines of this play spoiled and my artists insulted by your rude behaviour'.

After the nut-cracking incident the rest of the evening went strictly according to plan, with most first-night nerves controlled, if not conquered. Following the main play, as was common at the time, a short comedietta was performed, with songs by one Lucy Hawthorne. With a judiciously packed audience shouting for a speech from one of the company, Charles Dillon (never one to avoid a potentially emotional moment) stepped forward. He proceeded to thank all those who had made the evening possible, expressed a little pride in his achievements, and advised all those who had enjoyed the occasion to tell their friends as quickly as possible.

The *Era* seemed to be obsessed with the theatre's appearance, noting that:

The outside of the building we must describe as ugly in the extreme, but the interior presents a very pretty and attractive appearance. The Theatre, which it is estimated will accommodate about one thousand, has been built by Messrs David G. Laing and Sons, from designs and under the direction of the well known Mr James George Buckle, A.R.I.B.A., of Adam Street, Adelphi. The lines of the house are so arranged that a good view of the stage is obtained from every seat, and the auditorium is ventilated by means of a sunlight and large extraction cowl over the gallery.

Almost as an afterthought the reviewer wrote of the leading lady: 'Her presence was very attractive, and a sergeant of police who took a seat next to us remarked in confidence, "If that 'ed of 'air's hall 'er hown, sir, it's a very fine one and she ought to be proud on it".'

Seeds of doubt and words of warning were contained in a slightly patronizing piece by the influential *Stratford Express:*

The so-called Theatre Royal, Stratford, has been opened this week. We are not aware of any solid ground for the adoption of the 'Royal' title and if this is a prophecy it is a rather hardy one. If it is used to give an impression that the management desires to give only good plays and to make the theatre really desirable to Stratford, we hail the promise with pleasure. And it is only fair to admit that the new theatre has on the whole commenced very well. 'Richelieu' to begin with, 'Belphegor' next week, and a distinct promise given that a number of other 'legitimate' dramas shall be played – these are things which do certainly show a determination to appeal to the best instincts of playgoers and to make the theatre a home for the drama as distinguished from the dreary pieces in which the uninstructed delight – to witness a murder every twenty minutes. With the large population around it, and the far greater population which can easily reach it by rail, the Stratford Theatre Royal appears to have a very good chance of becoming a financial success, and at the same time conciliating the good opinion of many who now look upon the venture with coldness and doubt.

The contemporary press's doubts aside, and the Theatre Royal's relationship with the media has always been an ambivalent one, the inescapable fact was that those who had poured scorn on the idea of building a theatre in the area had been roundly defeated; it was now up to Charles Dillon, his actors and the community to exploit the victory.

Stratford as a town dates back to the early Middle Ages when it was known by the name of Stratford Langthorne. Situated on one of the most important routes from Essex to London it would have been a watering place for many a traveller, and it is tempting to speculate about Chaucerian knights or Jacobean actors refreshing themselves after a long trip from East Anglia. The city walls are a few miles to the west; east a little are the old sites of Barking and Wanstead. And it is the latter which was the country residence of the melancholy Earl of Essex, the man who launched a hopeless rebellion against Queen Elizabeth, but not before watching a special performance of Shakespeare's *Richard II*.

Stratford Bow is mentioned in the works of Thomas Dekker, and it is certain that the area would have had some theatrical pedigree by the first quarter of the seventeenth century. Puritan party dominance in the business sectors of London from the late 1560s ensured that almost all places of mass entertainment were located outside the city. Hence the 'Theatre' was built in Shoreditch in 1576 and the 'Curtain' was established nearby. When 'God's chosen' Calvinists came to power after the civil war all the theatres in London, and those discovered elsewhere, were closed down. The result was that the districts east of London were frequented by people of the theatre; and by the nineteenth century the tradition was established, with a whole chain of music-halls and small venues from Aldgate to Bow.

In terms of size and population the town remained relatively static, with a small commercial gardening industry accounting for the employment of something like twelve per cent of its inhabitants by the early 1880s. But with the coming of the steam age Stratford was transformed. In 1847 the Eastern Counties Railway built its magnificent depot, which by the middle of the century was the biggest repair yard in Europe. Inevitably jobs, people and houses followed in quick succession. The fruit and vegetable market grew accordingly, becoming the largest outside Covent Garden, and due to the cheapness of land, ambitious Victorian businessmen moved in to take advantage of expanding consumerism. In the thirty years after 1851 the population grew from under 19,000 to almost 129,000.

When the West Ham (incorporating Stratford) Local Board made its application to the authorities to be listed as a borough it could accurately state that:

> The growth of West Ham during the last twenty years is unprecedented in the annals of parochial history in this country, and in the result, a great rural district, much of which was marshland below the river level, has been converted into a populous and prosperous town, standing, with regard to population ninth on the list of all the large towns and cities of England and Wales.

What the statement omitted to mention was the subsequent growth of leisure-time and the failure of expanding towns to take account of the fact. The largely upper-working-class population of Stratford made ample use of the public houses in the area — many are the tales of East London streets dotted with children taking home jugs of beer to their parents — but this was far from sufficient. The church or chapel was still a significant meeting place in the 1880s and of course the middle classes had their pianos to sing around; there was, however, no theatre or music-hall within a convenient distance.

Another powerful impetus for the building of a theatre came from the sizable community of Jews who had fled from persecution in Russia, Poland and Lithuania and had settled in the East End of London from the late 1870s onwards. They had an old and noble history of the performing arts and brought this tradition with them to Britain. Although the main Jewish ghetto was in Whitechapel they also lived as far east as East Ham. For both Jews and gentiles in Stratford the best theatre on offer was the occasional travelling company or amateur project. Neither was satisfactory. One man who set out to fill this vacuum was Charles Dillon.

From contemporary photographs Dillon, with a full moustache and fashionable quiff, looks very much the combination of gentleman and charismatic rogue which was the essence of the Victorian success story. His real name was Silver, and its probable that he changed it due to admiration for the actor-manager W. Charles Dillon. Silver had played many of the same parts as his hero, both in Britain and on a tour of Australia. His mother had been an actress and his sister, who sometimes performed in the theatre, had married into the actor-manager family of the Fredericks. Both brother and sister appeared in local East London venues and in the small mobile theatres which toured Essex.

Relatively little is known of the man before 5 July 1884, when he applied to a slightly bemused collection of local magistrates for a licence to build a theatre in the middle of Stratford. He was supported by the business community for obvious reasons; the local press was far from hostile and the population at large greeted the news with enthusiasm. There was opposition, however, and it came with a vengeance from a churchman by the name of the Rev. R.P. Pelly, vicar of St John's, Stratford. He claimed to speak 'on behalf of all the clergy, Non-conformist ministers, Catholic priests, various employers of labour and local school-teachers' and referred to the poor being forced to steal money to enable them to attend sinful theatres.

The *Stage* covered the argument as follows:

He [the Rev. R.P. Pelly] produced a petition against it, signed by the clergy of the district, and urged 'that a theatre would not tend to the moral elevation of the people of the neighbourhood'; that it would injuriously affect a home close by; and that 'probably a low class of drama would be provided, so that it would become the resort of the lowest classes'. The intolerance of such one-sided arguments was at once apparent to the justices, and Colonel Howard, the chairman, met the clerical opposition boldly by saying 'the bench had a duty to perform to the public'. The licence for the new theatre was therefore granted, on the usual terms of being renewed annually. In arriving at this decision the justices expressed an opinion that a 'well conducted theatre would be a benefit to the neighbourhood.

With official permission granted, Dillon chose and obtained as a site a wheelwright's shop in Salway Road owned by a James Foster. By using the frame of the shop, the cost of building the theatre was estimated at £3,000, and the time demanded roughly twelve weeks. The choice of architect was James George Buckle, a leading man of the day who was later to write the highly regarded *Theatre Construction and Maintenance*. Buckle was regarded as an exponent of simple style in architecture, and his approach with the Theatre Royal was to structure a large part of the building inside the existing skeleton. Unfortunately, a critical surveyor did not approve of the idea, claiming that 'the conversion of Foster's shop by merely adding a ring of brick work to the outer wall was altogether unsafe and improper'.

The *Stratford Express* vented its views on the entire exploit:

If anyone who left Stratford thirty years ago were to learn that it was proposed to erect a permanent theatre there, he would not be a little startled we fancy. Stratford, as he would have known it, was very far indeed from being large enough to support a theatre, and indeed it is not so very long since people thought that two theatres were amply sufficient for London. Now the number of London theatres is almost past finding out, and only the cabmen and the Lord Chamberlain know where they all are.

The article went on to give the history of the enterprise, and concluded with:

We may therefore look forward to the early opening of a Stratford theatre. It is merely a question of time. It was certain that a permanent theatre must come before long, and it must be obvious that a permanent theatre is one over which the Justices can exercise a much more efficient control than they can exert over those itinerant companies which come to Stratford and don the buskins for a week or two every now and then.

Echoing the newspaper's words, a second report was submitted to the surveyor's department and this time was accepted with the proviso that another gallery exit was included. This requirement was deemed necessary following a spate of fires in large meeting places and a growing awareness among local councils of their civic responsibilities. Charles Dillon, always the optimist, announced that the grand opening of his theatre would be on 6 December. It was never to be. And a little shamefaced he informed the interested parties that they would now have to wait until Wednesday 17 December to view the Theatre Royal Stratford East.

After the first night it was inevitable that some of those at the theatre would feel a sense of anti-climax. Not so Charles Dillon. He fully realized that if Stratford East had any realistic chance of survival, a large and loyal following would have to be established within the first year. Following *Richelieu* came productions of *The Loan of a Lover Proof*, *The Lady of Lyons*, *The Duke's Motto* and *East Lynne* – all perennially popular and to be performed time and time again at Stratford. During the run of *The Duke's Motto* Dillon's zealousness resulted in a sword wound which kept him away from the theatre for a week, but his loss of blood did not seem to dampen his ardour. By May of the following year a different play was being performed each night. In one memorable week *Don Caesar de Bazan*, *The Shaughran*, *Hamlet*, *Romeo and Juliet*, *Richard III*, *The Devil in Paris*, *Richelieu* and *Chevalier St George* played. The companies at this time were composed of individual touring groups and local actors with something of a following. As a sign of goodwill their fees were raised to the princely sum of 1s 6d (7½p) per night.*

However energetic Dillon and his management staff may have been, the people of Stratford and the theatregoers of East London were not responding. One problem was the cumbersome sets and the difficulties of changing them with any rapidity. Dillon tried to overcome this by strictly limiting the design changes which proved to be a drastically short-sighted policy. Another hurdle was the audience's attitude to renderings of Shakespearean plays. Hamlet's

---

*A touching story of one of the men who trod the boards of Stratford East before the turn of the century concerns Jesmond Johnston. Born in Newcastle in 1874, he found his way south as a teenager, appeared at the Theatre Royal, and died at the appallingly young age of twenty-four. He was virtually forgotten until a historian descendent researched him, and donated a seat at the theatre in his name and memory.

advice to the Player King would not have gone amiss in most theatres of the 1880s, and when a gory *Richard III* or pompous *King Lear* was at Stratford East the takings dropped badly.

Criticisms of the management (Dillon's insistence on the classics was not always popular) and a realization that acting was less troublesome than organizing, made Dillon see the wisdom of going on tour in the final week of May 1885. He left the theatre in the hands of Fred Thomas, an actor of the old school who had retired in comfort to his tobacconist's shop in Stratford Broadway. As a local character Thomas was liked and trusted by the players, but under his management the theatre underwent the first of its many crises. With Dillon away, and many of the better company actors with him, Stratford East became a venue for touring groups which were seldom of the highest quality.

The first show under the new management consisted of a one-week run of *Uncle Tom's Cabin*, advertised as including 'Real Negroes – Bloodhounds – The Trick Donkey "Mike" – Acrobats – Banjoists and Bone Soloists'. And if the selection sounds a little bizarre, it should be remembered that for most people a 'real' negro was probably as rare a sight as the 'Trick Donkey "Mike"'. The local press reported nearly nine hundred people being turned away on the opening night, and thought that the 'deaths of little Eva and Uncle Tom were very pathetic scenes'. The rest of the short season was not as popular, and midway through September Dillon returned with a set of performers recruited on his travels in London and the provinces.

But despite optimism from a refreshed and seemingly rejuvenated manager, all was not well. By the time of the theatre's first birthday, the best the company could offer was a dubiously received *Dick Turpin* and a pantomime production of *Robinson Crusoe* written by a member of the cast. Ironically, due to the larger group of actors needed to perform these uninspiring plays the stalls and circle prices were raised by sixpence.

As audiences began to decline the state of the theatre and the morale of its members steadily dropped. Music-halls and small venues to the west were now attracting local people; the novelty of Stratford East had worn off. This was also a period of economic depression, and what money there was available was not spent on watching dowdy acts performed in a now lifeless theatre. In 1886, after attacks by the press and adverse comments by former allies, Charles Dillon decided to sell the establishment. With hindsight it is all too easy to dismiss Dillon as a man with some ambition but little vision. That would be a harsh and erroneous judgement. He was essentially a figure of the stage, not a person of business. Dillon's ultimate failure with the Theatre Royal should not diminish his importance as its creator and founder.

The man who took over was different from his predecessor in almost every respect. Albert O'Leary Fredericks was forty-six years old when he bought the theatre. A hard-headed businessman, he had made his money as a coal-merchant and had been partly financing Dillon's projects for some time. He was something of an eccentric, claimed (probably falsely) to have been born on the stage, and for most of his adult life dressed in dark and sombre clothes and was often mistaken for a clergyman. A £1,200 mortgage was raised from the builders of the theatre, David Laing and Sons, and £3,000 was given to Dillon to cover expenses and costs. With the theatre in his possession Fredericks lost no time in reappointing Fred Thomas as manager, and initiating a new and progressive policy.

The new approach consisted of combining the best in local and familiar talent with bigger and more prestigious West End names. Both Thomas and Fredericks realized the popularity of professionally produced melodramas, and neither man objected to catering for less sophisticated tastes. The *Stratford Express* evidently approved: 'The Easter programme has proved to have been a very satisfactory one. Great pains were taken by the management to meet the wishes of the public, and attracted by what promised to be good entertainment, the public have responded warmly, and good houses have been the rule.'

The repertoire for the second half of 1887 gives an example of the type of drama then offered at Stratford. In June Little Ada Reeve, a former child actress with a large following from her days in nearby Whitechapel, came to the theatre with her father to appear in *The Black Flag*. In September *Sentenced to Death, Sole Survivor* and *Brought to Justice* played successively to packed and delighted audiences. To add a taste of the exotic to the season Thomas then introduced the Diorama to the theatre. An ornate though far from perfect device, it was the precursor of the cinema and attracted people from all parts of East London. It was billed as 'Messrs Poole's Grand Dioramic Excursions' and visits were promised to 'the principal places, cities and scenes all over the world'. Supporting acts included such notables as Herr Blitz, 'the original plate charmer, manipulator and equiposier', and Mr Harry Stewart, 'the great American protean change artiste and vocalist'.

By the end of the year Fredericks was taking a more direct interest in the theatre, and after consultations proposed a series of architectural extensions. He bought property next door in Salway Road, knocked down a substantial part of it, and built new dressing-rooms and a workshop. The original changing facilities had been underneath the stage; they were inconvenient, subject to extremes of temperature and provoked constant complaints from actors. Only

11

weeks later Fred Thomas, the man who had quietly but capably maintained the theatre through hard times, resigned. Whether or not resignation was a euphemistic term is not clear, but as soon as Thomas had gone Fredericks appointed a new managerial team.

Hugh Moss, a playwright of modest reputation, was brought in as general manager of the theatre. Another author, Joseph Ellis, was given the combined position of stage and resident manager and Emily Fredericks (wife of the owner's brother and sister to Charles Dillon) became wardrobe mistress. At various times during the new administration other members of the Fredericks family would fill official positions. Seat prices were raised, bringing the financial potential of the theatre to £60 per night, and with the extra revenue the English Opera Company was brought to Stratford to perform *Faust* and *The Marriage of Figaro*. Their performances were greeted with surprising approval.

By the beginning of 1891 the theatre was on a firm financial footing, and Fredericks decided to take a lesson from his coal-trade days and reinvest the money. He bought property in Angel Lane which was at the back of the stage and built on a further twenty feet. An elaborate curtain depicting Pompeii before the volcano was put up, made by yet more members of the family, and for the first time offices were built for management staff. In addition two bars were installed, one for the dress circle and another for the pit and stalls.

For five years the theatre's repertoire maintained its balance of melodrama with occasional attempts at classical pieces. Although the works of Shaw, Wilde and Pinero were offered, local audiences were apparently addicted to the inestimable delights of *A Kiss in the Dark* or *Lost to the World*. A little disillusioned, Fredericks nevertheless took advantage of a development scheme undertaken by the West Ham Council and sought a lease for some land in the middle of Stratford High Street. With the council's blessing – by this time theatres had lost much of their notoriety – he set about building what was to be known rather grandiloquently as the Borough Theatre and Opera House. An ambitious series of productions was planned and an attempt was made to interest theatregoers who rarely wandered out of the confines of Shaftesbury Avenue. After the opening production one *Stratford Express* reporter found it difficult to contain his enthusiasm:

> that the event excited very great interest in the minds of the people of West Ham was evidenced by the crowded state of the thoroughfare near the theatre ever since the afternoon. When the time for opening approached the crowd became so great that the traffic was impeded, notwithstanding the vigilance of the police. Uniformed members of the Leyton and Leytonstone Fire

Charles Dillon: a little vision, much ambition but limited stamina

Albert Fredericks laid the structure for a
theatre for all seasons

2

Edwardian lady, modern influence: Caroline
Ellis Fredericks

3

Sam Fredericks: all in the family

Katie Fredericks in a feline pose

5

J. Rowland Sales – never had a chance

6

Brigade with detachments from a number of other similar institutions were formed up outside the chief entrance and along the road forming a way for theatre bound vehicles to pass through. This, in addition to presenting a picturesque spectacle, was a wise precautionary measure, for otherwise the drivers would have found considerable difficulty in forcing a passage to the doors. To avoid as much as possible an unpleasant crush, the doors were early thrown open, with the result that in a very short space of time the cheaper parts of the house were crowded . . . As is customary the theatre was but dimly lighted before the commencement of the performance. Thus much of the beauty of the decoration was invisible until the performance began. Suddenly without any note of warning, the theatre became a blaze of light as every electric arc flashed simulataneously, setting forth all the beauty of the theatre; simultaneously the tapestry curtain was drawn from the front of the stage, disclosing to view the magnificent act drop representing Epping Forest. Immediately the orchestra struck up the National Anthem, the audience rising en masse. Scarcely had the last note been struck ere the house burst into a storm of applause – a perfect furore which defies description, and which was some minutes before it subsided.

The new theatre managed to attract sufficiently large audiences to remain solvent, but before long all initial hopes to extend the West End to Stratford had been relinquished. After the 1896 local elections the Borough Theatre's problems became more acute. Fredericks was elected as a councillor of the Stratford ward – his success may well have been due to his popularity among railway workers because they had been allowed to use the theatre for meetings.[*] His political success, however, brought him into direct conflict with the East London Temperance movement, which had long opposed the theatre.

With the backing of Non-conformist churches and large sections of the new middle classes and through intensive lobbying, the Temperance organization became a powerful force exerting its influence nationally from the 1850s. In the East End it was particularly vociferous, and its entreaties made it impossible for Fredericks to obtain a drinks licence for his new theatre. Once on the council he tried to reform the alcohol regulations, but his opponents brought pressure to bear and carried the day by a healthy majority. Not happy with a 'dry' theatre, Fredericks offered, without success an extra £500 on the lease if the stipulations were amended.

There was an inevitable clash of interests between the Theatre Royal and the

[*]This arrangement was continued until the 1950s – the heyday of Theatre Workshop.

Borough Theatre and Opera House, with both venues competing for audiences. Fredericks's hopes that a broader London public would come and support the new venture simply did not materialize. It also became apparent that whatever difficulties the Theatre Royal had experienced in the past, it did now have a small but loyal following. As interest in the Borough Theatre slackened, Fredericks's investment diminished and he subsequently gave up any idea of channelling the best productions into the newer theatre. The Borough Theatre gradually turned into an occasional venue, was closed for prolonged periods and was finally transformed into a cinema. Though not suffering the ignominy of living out its final days as a bingo hall, it now stands derelict.

Anxious to stress his commitment to the Theatre Royal, in April 1897 Fredericks arranged a grand reopening under the title of the 'Theatre Royal and Palace of Varieties'. 'A crowded audience occupied the Theatre Royal on Monday evening,' wrote the *Stratford Express*, 'when for the first time a variety performance was given. It was somewhat strange to see smoking in the auditorium, but the audience quickly adapted themselves to the altered conditions, and everything passed off pleasantly enough and quite successfully'. Three more variety evenings were produced in the following weeks, until in June Willie Fredericks, died suddenly. He was Albert's nephew and was of paramount importance in the running of the theatre.

The death of his relative, friend and adviser had a profound influence on Fredericks. After a closure of the theatre as a sign of respect, a new man was brought in. The description, 'Palace of Varieties', was dropped and less informal productions were once more staged. Fredericks's involvement with the theatre became more relaxed in the following months, until finally, he was elected as a Labour alderman in 1898. Although he was always available to give advice and never missed a first night the Theatre Royal was no longer his passion. On 26 June 1901 he died, and was buried only a few miles from the theatre in Leytonstone's Catholic cemetery. If Charles Dillon had conceived the theatre, Albert Fredericks had been its saviour.

Control stayed in the hands of the family, with Caroline Fredericks Ellis taking over the management. Almost immediately she began a process of modernization, spending over £5,000 on introducing electricity and giving the entire building a now long overdue facelift. She also brought more commercial acts to Stratford, including the intriguingly named 'Little Dolly – the smallest barefoot sand dancer in the world' and 'Dr Walford Bodie – the bloodless surgeon'. To complete the season, there was a show of bioscope pictures and a range of competitions was organized by the theatre for local people. By 1914 Stratford East was firmly established as the theatre of working people from

West Ham and urban Essex. It had come through periods of stagnation and slump, but it had survived. And then the lamps went out all over Europe.

Initially the strange death of liberal England seemed to have relatively little effect on the theatre. While empires were being destroyed and whole armies smashed the only concession Stratford East made to the war was to raise its prices. But the end of the war brought with it profound social change and places of entertainment realized that unless they took account of the fact they would find themselves without audiences. From the death of Caroline Fredericks Ellis in 1919 to the early twenties the theatre barely remained in existence. And on Bank Holiday Monday in August 1921 it was damaged by fire.

> Considerable excitment prevailed in the neighbourhood of the Theatre Royal on Monday night when it was discovered that the building was on fire [the *Stratford Express* informed its readers]. There had been the usual performances during the evening and when the audience left everything was as usual. At about midnight, however, smoke was seen issuing from the stage end of the theatre and the West Ham Fire Brigade was immediately called both by a stranger and by the night staff of the telephone exchange opposite, who had seen the glare oı the flames. A general call to the West Ham Fire Brigade station was given and three motor pumps and two escapes were quickly in attendance.
>
> On their arrival the firemen found the stage and scenery were involved, and the stage area enveloped by dense clouds of smoke. The value of the safety curtain was demonstrated by the fact that it had prevented the fire from spreading to the auditorium. The firemen experienced considerable difficulty in combating the fire because of the dense smoke, but they concentrated their efforts upon the flames spreading to the hall and in this they were entirely successful . . . it was three and a half hours before they were able to leave the scene.

The damage forced the theatre to close its doors until January of the following year. When it was reopened the programme seemed trite and out of touch to an East London people in the middle of an economic depression. The management displayed a curious obsession with the Latter Day Saints, putting on *The Mormon and his Wives, A Mormon's Favourite Wife* and *A Mormon's Bride.* While theatres all over the country were competing with an expanding broadcasting network, at Stratford the classic melodrama was still the mainstay of the programme. In his unpublished autobiography Willian Rumsey, a driver's assistant in Canning Town before the Second World War, describes a typical evening at the theatre in the twenties.

Almost opposite the depot was the Theatre Royal and as a local newspaper stated, this theatre was considered by the traders of the Angel Lane market as their theatre. Monday was the day when the market closed. The traders would clean up their yards and take their empty sacks and boxes back to Stratford Market, then like myself would go to the Royal for an evening's entertainment – and we all got it.

All the old melodramas were played like *Maria Marten and the Red Barn, Tod Slaughter the Demon Barber* and a number of such plays, but no play was successful unless in the cast was a typical villain that had to be dressed in black with a black cape, a very long moustache and a must – a black top hat, for the following reason: only the innocent and foolhardy would sit in the middle of the front row. The 'orchestra' would be protected, especially over the top with small meshed wire netting.

Everything went smoothly until the villain, decked out as explained above, wanted to take the virginal daughter of the farmer who couldn't pay the rent of the farm. As the poor girl was crying 'No, no, help me' this demon would put his hands on her shoulders, this was the signal for action from the audience. Over would go a barrage of rotten fruit and tomatoes that had been put in readiness to save the wench's honour. The target was that black hat. This black demon would make a hasty retreat, the girl unsullied and the farmer got away without paying up the arrears. On one occasion this wolf in sheep's clothing strangled his victim, lifted up the body in his arms, walked to the footlights and with a tearful voice (said) 'What shall I do with the body?' One piece of advice was physically impossible, another could not be carried out in public. All suggestions were accompanied with language which was not parliamentary.

By 1926 the theatre was existing virtually only on melodramas. In May, in the week of the General Strike, it closed. Between the end of that year and 1932 no advertising was taken out in the local press, the profile of the theatre was extremely low, and, according to local historian Oscar Tapper, the owners may have considered turning the theatre into a cinema, as had been done with the Borough (the Rex Cinema from 1933). The thirties were difficult times for the theatre everywhere, but dockside Stratford was particularly badly affected during that period. All the Theatre Royal could possibly do was sit tight and wait for the economic storm to subside.

In 1932 the theatre was reopened with a season of variety acts, most of which were appallingly staged and badly performed. After only five weeks a lack of support from the community forced another closure. There was a gap of almost two years before Stratford East received a new injection of interest. At the beginning of 1935 an ex-Royal Navy officer by the name of John Williams introduced a series of productions – in which his wife, Ivy Maurice, usually took a leading role – which earned him the title locally of the 'King of Melodrama'. Even though the company was willing to change its repertoire every other day the programme was, however, not a success.

By the summer the theatre was open to any touring company prepared to fill it; by the following year Williams, by now supported by friends after having lost over £3,000, was summonsed as a debtor to Bow Court. In July the theatre was in the hands of new management, and the *Stratford Express* stated that:

> The former patrons of the Theatre Royal in Angel Lane, Stratford, will learn with interest that the building is to shortly re-open for the presentation of good class variety and revue attractions. The new lessee is Mr R.E. O'Brien who has had a long experience in the theatrical world. The theatre is being re-seated, re-decorated inside and out and the opening date is Bank Holiday Monday.

In fact the anticipated season never actually happened. O'Brien disappeared and control of the theatre passed to Frank Selway Dunsford and John Southern (both with long theatrical experience) and a musical programme began with a production entitled *Going Gay*. For the first time at Stratford small gifts were given to members of the audience as a method of increasing patronage – this was already familiar procedure at cinemas – and enterprising teenagers obtained several cigarette cases by discovering an alternative route into the theatre by a side door.

> So great was the interest in the re-opening of the Theatre Royal [announced the *Stratford Express*] that hundreds of people who hoped to gain admission for the first performances were disappointed. A considerable time before the doors opened queues began to form and the building was quickly filled to capacity. There was an even larger 'crush' for the second house. In all its long history the theatre could not have had a more enthusiastic send off.

This was an optimistic piece of journalism. By December 1938 the theatre was once again under new management, that of Leslie Vyner. But the Blitz hit the East Thames area very hard indeed, and Vyner never had the chance to prove himself. The theatre remained closed until 1943.

The man who was to take the theatre over had been involved in live entertainment for most of his adult life. J. Rowland Sales had begun as an actor in 1907, became the youngest West End manager at twenty and proceeded to work as a producer, agent and promoter until he came to Stratford East. He aimed to appeal directly to local audiences but, as the following advertising letter to the public demonstrates, his attitudes were completely outdated.

Having now successfully launched your Stratford Theatre I feel, on behalf of my co-Directors and self, that you should know that we had very great difficulties in getting the Theatre reopened and running, and at times it seemed almost impossible to surmount the various obstacles we encountered.

In the first place you know that the Theatre has a fine old tradition and I am glad to say we are now building up a good clientele by giving you the very best attractions procurable.

The Revues you have seen up to now including 'Hi Diddle Diddle', 'Bearskins and Blushes', 'Swing Inn', 'Yes Please', 'Show Folk', 'Blaze Away', 'Lovelies and Laughter', 'Young Ideas', 'Slap Happy Road Show', are only a few of the first class companies that have appeared at the Theatre and for the future we have still better shows booked including 'Yodels and Yells', 'Miss Camouflage', 'Q for Fun', 'Nights of Jazz' and 'Women are Wonderful'. All these shows are 100% Revues appearing at all the best London and Provincial Theatres. We shall continue to submit for your approval, during the coming months, the very best entertainment that can be offered, and owing to the strong Public demand the Theatre will remain open during the Summer months, and, as you will notice from our publicity matter, although the Entertainment Tax was raised on May 16th, we have not put up our prices. They are popular summer prices, viz.: 3/–, 2/6, 2/–, 2/3, 1/9 and 1/– all including tax and all reservable . . .

As you know our opening took place on March 29th, at which His Worship the Mayor Alderman A.W. Wells, J.P. graciously performed the opening ceremony and it has given us the greatest encouragement possible to see the interest the Public have taken. Our policy is a progressive one and we feel sure that you, our Patrons will continue the support you are giving us each week.

Lastly, we shall be pleased to welcome any suggestions from you also for our first Grand Annual Christmas Pantomime. Please addrress communications to the Manager. This is *your Theatre* and we welcome your co-operation in all details.

Don't forget our fully licensed Bars, all goods of the very finest quality at popular prices.

Lastly, we are giving you DEFINITE VALUE FOR MONEY at this Theatre, and conduct it for your pleasure and amusement, thus meriting your continued support.

But Sales's period as manager was not a runaway success. After flirting with the idea of making the theatre a dance-hall and failing to prevent months of closure, Stratford East was left from the end of the war until the winter of 1946 dark, empty and on the verge of collapse.

David Horne was the next candidate for failure and obscurity. With his Eton, Sandhurst and the Grenadier Guards background he represented an entirely different type of manager. He had joined his father's touring company in the twenties, acted with the Old Vic and later with ENSA and had appeared throughout the country. After taking control on October 1946 he set about changing the structure of the theatre, bringing it up to date and repairing the damage inflicted by neglect and German bombers. Most of the electric power supply was reinstalled, the seating was completely changed and a new bar selling non-alcoholic drinks was fitted.

The opening night production, in November, was Pinero's *The Second Mrs Tanqueray*, followed by Shaw's *Pygmalion* and Arnold Bennett and Edward Knoblock's *Milestones*. The season was not unsuccessful, but there was still no breakthrough. In 1947 Horne decided to go on tour, and left his former publicity officer Geoffrey Hastings in charge. His period at the theatre was unexpectedly popular. A programme including Rattigan's *The Winslow Boy*, Coward's *Blithe Spirit* and *Fly Away Peter* — with a young Kenneth Williams in the cast — gave local audiences what they wanted: plays still popular in the West End and with contemporary significance and humour. But providing such drama was not an easy task. Stratford people were proving volatile, and in the summer of 1948 David Horne once again became the manager.

When he relaunched the theatre in the following year his plan was to introduce a series of guest stars in each play. The season was officially opened by Sybil Thorndike, and the first production was *Gaslight* with Derek Bond.

It was very strange indeed acting in a theatre which was surrounded by the results of bombing [remembers Bond] and it was clear that the entire management of the theatre were trying to capture the local people's imagination. It was a success, no doubt. But I think that even then one doubted whether Stratford could really support a theatre like that. There was an enormous character about the place, that much was certainly true.

After the first night audiences were again disappointing, lured away by the ever improving television service and the cinema which was undergoing heavy investment both in Britain and the United States. Although devoting much time and energy to Stratford, Horne lost a great deal of money and failed to turn it into a viable concern.

The theatre closed again, and opened in December 1949 under the temporary management of Gabriel Toyne and Diana Beaumont. Both had acted in the past and had been involved in theatrical administration. It was during their period at Stratford East that a little-known touring company from the North of England called Theatre Workshop came for a week to perform their *Alice in Wonderland*. Although lack of interest on the part of local people prevented a longer stay, those seven days were enough to enable the members of that group to become familiar with a theatre and an area which was later to change their lives.

In January of the following year a small piece of history was made. Stratford's successful production of *Spring-heeled Jack, The Terror of Epping Forest* was the first play ever to be televised live. It is ironic that the very success of the enterprise hammered yet another nail into the coffin of post-war provincial theatre. After a twelve-week closure Phyllis Gow opened the theatre as a limited company, proposing to use it as an experimental venue for pre-West End shows. Diana Dors was one of the many young actors and actresses who played there, but by this time Stratford was virtually moribund.

Under a new management an attempt was made to produce revue and variety evenings, though by 1952 a collection of nude shows was the best Stratford could offer. Broadcaster and author Richard Baker was present at one such gathering.

> It was called something like 'Strip Strip Hooray' or 'All Off Tonight', and I don't really know why we went along. It was very scruffy; the orchestra consisted of about three people and the leader, if you can call him that, had to climb over the seats to get into place. I remember feeling something wet dripping onto my head, I looked up and saw someone squeezing a tomato from the circle.

By January 1953, and with a stage adaption of the *Daily Mirror* cartoon strip called *Jane Comes to Town* running, the theatre closed. Dozens of similar old and stately buildings throughout the country were being demolished, and the same fate would doubtless have befallen Stratford East, but for the fact that a radical drama group was booked to play for six weeks.

2.
All Roads Lead To E15

Theatre Workshop, the era of Joan Littlewood and Gerry Raffles and the events of the time are still shrouded in show business myth. In this chapter I intend to clear some of the ground and simply tell the facts.

The story of Theatre Workshop has its origins decades before the move to Stratford, beginning many miles from London and the prosperous South. The period of the late 1920s witnessed an upsurge in radical thought, following a horrific war, a failed general strike and the beginnings of international fascism. The Workers' Theatre Movement was dedicated to entertainment with a political message for working-class audiences. In the movement's wake came other groups and activists, among them a committed young man called Jimmy Miller. Later to change his name to Ewan MacColl, he helped to organize left-wing theatre groups in Salford and Manchester and much influenced by German and central European drama, was instrumental in forming the Theatre of Action in 1934. Its manifesto proclaimed its broad aims:

> The commercial theatre is limited by its dependence upon a small section of society which neither desires, nor dares to face the urgent and vital problems of today. The theatre, if it is to live, must of necessity reflect the spirit of the age. This spirit is found in the social conflicts which dominate world history today − in the ranks of 3,000,000 unemployed, starving for bread, while wheat is burned for fuel.
>
> The Theatre of Action realizes that the very class which plays the chief part in contemporary history − the class upon which the prevention of war and the defeat of reaction solely depends − is debarred from expression in the present-day theatre. This theatre will perform, mainly in working-class districts, plays which express the life and struggles of the workers. Politics, in its fullest sense, means the affairs of the people. In this sense, the plays

23

done will be political. The members of the Theatre of Action are actors and actresses, producers, writers, scene-designers and other active supporters of its aims. All interested in its work are invited to become members of the Theatre of Action at a monthly subscription of 6d.

MacColl was joined by a charismatic young woman from Stockwell, Joan Littlewood, who as a sixteen-year-old orphan had run away from school before winning a scholarship to the Royal Academy of Dramatic Art. At this time the pair were still formulating their ideas, based around what Howard Goorney, author of *The Theatre Workshop Story*, describes as:

A combination of being acutely aware of the issues of the time, the development of a new language in theatre which working people could follow and appreciate, a completely modern form of movement as yet hardly used on the stage and quite simply a high degree of skill and expertise in all of the theatrical disciplines.

These ideas and the way they were expressed brought the Theatre of Action into direct conflict with the conventional wisdom of the hard left of the period. Unity Theatre, supported by many in the Communist and Labour parties, believed in a form of socialist realism in their work. The following of any party line was a complete anathema to MacColl and Littlewood and several of the comments made by ardent young communists – 'You would be much better off selling the *Daily Worker* rather than putting on plays' – produced a division. While the Theatre of Action looked to the biomechanics of Meyerhold and the dancing actor theories of Laban and Bodenwiser, others on the left seemed to believe that J.V. Stalin was as knowledgeable on theatre as he was on the treatment of *kulaks*.

Now resident in Manchester, they set about producing a mammoth rendering of Hans Chlumberg's *Miracle at Verdun*. With the co-operation of the Peace Pledge Union, whose initial idea it had been, students and volunteer actors were assembled to provide the cast. The performances were successful, but the stringent demands made of those taking part forced many in the group to drop out. The remaining members re-formed in a body called Theatre Union, recruiting new actors and helpers (including Harold Lever, later Treasury Financial Secretary to Harold Wilson) and issued the following declaration of intent and purpose:

The theatre must face up to the problems of its time; it cannot ignore the poverty and human suffering which increases every day. It cannot, with sincerity, close its eyes to the disasters of its time: means-test suicides, wars, fascism and the million sordid accidents reported in the daily press. If the theatre of today would reach the heights achieved 4,000 years ago in Greece and 400 years ago in Elizabethan England it must face up to such problems. To those who say that such affairs are not the concern of the theatre or that the theatre should confine itself to treading the paths of 'beauty' and 'dignity', we would say 'Read Shakespeare, Marlowe, Webster, Sophocles, Aeschylus, Aristophanes, Calderon, Molière, Lope de Vega, Schiller and the rest'. The Theatre Union says that in facing up to the problems of our time and by intensifying our efforts to get at the essence of reality, we are also attempting to solve our own theatrical problems both technical and ideological. By doing this we are ensuring the future of the theatre, a future which will not be born in the genteel atmosphere of retirement and seclusion, but rather in the clash and turmoil of the battles between the oppressors and the oppressed.

One of the first major productions of the new organization was Hasek's *The Good Soldier Schweik,* offering MacColl ample opportunity to put his theories into practice. The adaptation of the play used was that by Bertolt Brecht and Erwin Piscator, the set designs and lighting were revolutionary and when the company played in the Lesser Free Trade Hall the results were better than anybody had dared hope for. Howard Goorney became passionately involved with the group in 1938:

The atmosphere was very optimistic, it seemed that everything would turn out fine in the end, we'd conquer the world because we knew what we were doing and the working class would rise up and support us [he explained]. We were naive. Not about our work but about the situation. Gradually we painfully realized that without resources, without any money, it was not going to be easy. The entire group would be depressed, and then we'd play somewhere like a Butlin's holiday camp and a couple of thousand people would love us.

Joan was the driving force. She was remarkable. Remarkable. She was also subject to extreme changes of mood: from being in a state of complete exaltation she would start the most terrible rows, absolutely appalling ones, seemingly over nothing. She had this curious reluctance to own anything. If ever we were given a gift, and that happened quite often when things were really bad, by the end of the week Joan's would be with somebody else. She made a lot of mistakes, she was also a genius.

Littlewood's influence steadily frew from the late thirties, becoming apparent in the Theatre Union's productions of *The Masters of Time*, a Russian play about the Bolshevik revolution and *Last Edition*, a theatrical newspaper which resulted in a legal prosecution. But as the Second World War loomed, the maintenance of an organized drama group became virtually impossible.

But the war did see the emergence of Gerry Raffles. Optimistic, tenacious and likeable he had come from a comfortable Russo-Jewish family which had established itself in the northern garment trade. Whereas Ewan MacColl had taken on the mantle of policy administrator or, as one contemporary termed it, 'political commissar', Raffles saw himself as a businessman who could function at his best inside the theatre. He also began a relationship with Joan Littlewood which, for many, came to represent the very essence of Theatre Workshop.

By the end of the war a new circle of people had joined the group, and having raised a sum of around £400 from personal accounts and loans they felt confident enough to launch a new season of productions. The town chosen as their base was Kendal, and, ironically, they settled in on one floor of the local Conservative Party Offices. Yet another manifesto was posted, the last paragraph of which stated that:

Theatre Workshop is an organization of artists, technicians and actors who are experimenting in stage-craft. Its purpose is to create a flexible theatre-art, as swift moving and plastic as the cinema, by applying the recent technical advances in light and sound, and introducing music and the 'dance theatre' style of production.

A lasting title had been found, it now remained for ideas to be put into practice.

The vehicle they chose was *Johnny Noble*, written by MacColl and heavily researched by Littlewood. It was a ballad opera, using all of the advanced ideas of lighting, design and movement which Theatre Workshop advocated to tell the story of a love affair in the 1930s. After opening in August 1945 to an enthusiastic reception, the play was taken on tour, and in October returned to Kendal to run with Federico García Lorca's *The Love of Don Perlimplin for Belisa in his Garden*. The repertoire was then expanded with a work which is as relevant and poignant today as it was in 1945: *Uranium 235* was performed during the months following the destruction of Hiroshima and Nagasaki, and it explored, and tried to explain, the nuclear question to a then uninformed public. The form of the piece was unconventional, the actors involved were pushed to their limits, and its impact was immense.

The theatre also managed to recruit a new wave of young enthusiasts, among whom were actors and technicians who were to remain with Workshop for many years. Rosalie Williams stayed with the company throughout its hardest days, as did David Scase. One member, John Bury, known as 'Camel' (his childhood nickname) due to an excess of Johns in the company, provided revolutionary and usually outstanding sets for the production; he went on to become the National Theatre's head of design.

The Workshop found a more permanent home in the middle of 1946 when a theatre lover donated one wing of Ormesby Hall just outside of Middlesbrough. The main advantage of the location was space; for the first time in what seemed like years the Workshop players could rehearse in relative comfort and try out new routines, methods and disciplines. By August of the following year a short season was produced at the Manchester Library Theatre, featuring the successful *Johnny Noble* and *The Flying Doctor,* adapted from Molière's *Le Médecin malgré lui.* But financial pressures were catching up with the company, and after a series of dates in London and Brighton the only course open was a brief disbandment.

When they did reassemble it was largely due to the fact that Gerry Raffles had been able to settle the vast bulk of the company's debts. In his book on Theatre Workshop Howard Goorney refused to speculate on where the money came from; all we do know is that Raffles's concerned and generous father had helped out in the past. By March 1948 Workshop was back in a Manchester house, beginning work on Ewan MacColl's new play, *The Other Animals.* A little later an American heavy bomber which was carrying packages of equipment for entertainments for the troops crashed in Derbyshire. After some organized scavenging, John Bury and his helpers managed to secure enough of the load to see Workshop through for some years.

The Other Animals finally opened at the Library Theatre in July. Essentially a difficult, esoteric piece, it was reviewed generously enough by the critics but was greeted a little less enthusiastically by the public. What *The Other Animals* demonstrated above all was the unique potential of Theatre Workshop. With the help of company member Kristin Lind and faithful supporter Tom Driberg, an attempt to enlarge that potential was made by touring the still devastated post-war Czechoslavakia. The sojourn lasted for some ten weeks, and was probably the setting for an often repeated and invariably distorted Workshop anecdote. During the journey in between performances an actor searching for an unnamed possession on the floor of a bus came across a contraceptive. An inquiry was immediately undertaken to discover who it belonged to, not because of any moral outrage, but bewilderment as to who could afford it!

On returning from Europe another house in Manchester was found, and from here productions of *The Flying Doctor,* Chekhov's *The Proposal* and a second season of *Perlimplin* were launched. For the Christmas tour of that year Joan

Littlewood worked on a stage version of *Alice in Wonderland,* and it was during this run that Workshop first came into contact with the Theatre Royal, Stratford East. Contrary to what many of the company members may have said afterwards, the run-down and generally dilapidated venue made no real impression at all. Furthermore, the tour had run into more financial trouble.

For the next few months, while touring in completely inadequate conditions and appearing on poorly equipped and sometimes dangerous stages, there were frequent arguments and periods of gloom. Although a systematic approach had been adopted to establish a revolutionary form of theatre, struggling to remain solvent and working in village halls and schools was not what everybody had joined for. A full season of school appearances was undertaken with Joan Littlewood's witty adaption of *A Midsummer Night's Dream,* and this was followed by a tour in Norway and Sweden. In early 1952 Harry H. Corbett joined the divided group. Tired of playing artificial characters in provincial repertory theatre, he embraced Workshop and its founders with a passion. But the infusion of young and refreshing talent did not counter a prevalent sense of frustration.

Productions in Scotland (where Workshop was accepted from the very beginning,) and Brighton again received glowing notices; but, as Howard Goorney remembers, a nadir had been reached.

> Quite extraordinary. When we played we would be congratulated, audiences would enthuse about us and usually critics would be more than encouraging. But you can only take so much squalor, and it really was squalor. Some members wanted to build individual reputations, after all they were getting older, and others lost interest. There was also the fact that we weren't getting our message across to enough people by moving from house to house, and borrowing as we went. A move had to happen.

As luck would have it a relatively obscure theatre in the East End of London fell vacant at this time, and Gerry Raffles was informed of the fact.

The decision to build a permanent home at the Theatre Royal Stratford East was far from unanimous. Opposition to the move was led and articulated by Ewan MacColl. He believed that by becoming resident in London the actions of Workshop would be unduly influenced by the critics and the theatre-going middle class. MacColl had always seen Theatre Workshop as an itinerant organization, and any argument that Stratford was at core a working-class community or that in the long term the critics simply did not matter, had no effect on him. After meeting in Glasgow the issue was settled; the move southwards would be made. MacColl resigned soon afterwards.

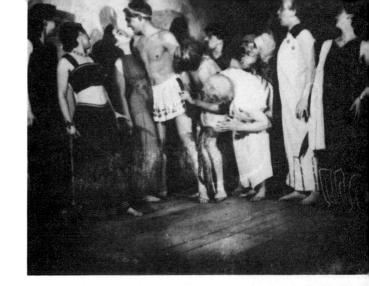

Theatre Union, Manchester 1941

7

The Flying Doctor, 1945 – Joan Littlewood
with arms folded

8

The 1948 tour of Czechoslovakia

9

The Dutch Courtesan, 1954

10

Good Soldier Schweik, 1955

11

The Green Room shortly after redecoration.
Littlewood talks to Murray Melvin and
Stephen Lewis

12

The Hostage, 1958

13

Murray Melvin in *The Hostage:*
his performance was a complete success

14

Harry Corbett—universally liked, universal
missed

15

After Ewan MacColl's departure Gerry Raffles, with Joan Littlewood, became increasingly dominant. With fellow Workshop member Harry Greene he made a dawn trip to Stratford to prepare the way for the rest of the company. When the bulk of the other actors and technicians arrived in January 1953 they were faced with a cold, damp theatre which hadn't seen a genuine success or any glamour for many years. With hardly any money, a mere shell of a venue and a few dozen hungry actors to feed and keep happy Littlewood and Raffles intended to take British theatre by storm. Manchester-born actress Avis Bunnage was to star in several of the theatre's most prestigious and influential productions. She reconnoitred Stratford East shortly after the visit of Gerry Raffles as she was already in East London searching for temporary accommodation.

I couldn't even get in through the main doors, I had to slip in at a little pass door at the side. It was so cold, so terribly cold. Everything was a dirty brown colour, there was no hot water and the entire theatre couldn't have been painted in years. I'd managed to get digs with Harry Corbett in West Ham for twenty-six shillings a week bed and breakfast, but before very long we were just too broke to afford it.

Some of the group had already moved straight into the theatre, they were sleeping in the dressing-rooms and either having their meals there or at a local café where the owners were quite sympathetic. I followed them. It wasn't for any idea of romanticism or togetherness, we were simply without any money at all. In a small room overlooking the railway station I cooked chips on a small ring in the corner, slept and lived there. But officially we weren't allowed to. So when the fire authorities arrived someone would announce over the tannoy that 'Walter Plinge is wanted on stage' and that would be the signal for us to hide the beds and get everything straight.

The first production, starting a two-week run on 2 February 1953, was *Twelfth Night*. With tired actors packed into every space and Ms Bunnage wearing a cardigan underneath her Jacobean low-cut dress (there was no heating), the play was seen by uncomfortable and unenthusiastic audiences. This was to be a period most Workshop devotees prefer not to remember when they reminisce. The average wage in the company was under £2 a week, and by the middle of the first season most of the members were living in the theatre on a diet of vitamin pills, benzedrine and coffee. Box office takings were their only income; it would be over two years before Theatre Workshop could afford to buy Stratford East.

A series of two-week runs was established, with *Juno and the Paycock, Arms and the Man, Anna Christie* and half a dozen other works playing until August when the company travelled up to the Edinburgh Festival to perform *Uncle Vanya* and *The Imaginary Invalid*. Although this was a difficult time there were, even as early as the first month of the 1953 season, devoted fans and supporters. Peggy Soundy, then an agricultural researcher in Ongar, was entranced by an early production at the theatre and began a supporter's club which at its peak had 2,000 members. She has strong memories of the time:

> Joan was obsessed with everybody being completely versatile. If you wanted to act, write, direct or whatever, first of all you had to paint and decorate and use a vacuum cleaner. It had two aims: it made actors feel what it was like to perform fairly menial tasks, and it was also the only way to keep the theatre in one piece.

Joan Littlewood used the early seasons at Stratford to develop her ideas. She had read, seen and studied Stanislavsky and Brecht and was certainly influenced by both; but her contribution was more than just a British adaption of European thought. Ken Hill, who took over the direction of the theatre after Gerry Raffles's death, believes that she 'invented the working-class actor'. Although her style was to change several times throughout the course of Theatre Workshop, she always believed in nurturing local, inevitably working-class, talent. Her top priority at Stratford was to stamp out 'acting in the past tense'. From the very first productions hardly any stage make-up was used, footlights were considered outmoded – largely due to the influence of John Bury – and the proscenium arch was never treated as anything other than an obstacle.

An emphasis on contemporary dance training and movement also played a central part in Littlewood's early approach. Maxwell Shaw had been a working actor for five years when he went to Stratford for an audition. The response and atmosphere he found at the Theatre Royal were different from anything he had encountered before.

> I'd been around, had a stack of audition pieces and considered myself to be pretty experienced. I read one, and Joan asked if I had anything else. This went on and on until I'd exhausted my repertoire. Then she asked me to do some improvisation, which I'd never done before, and after about forty minutes she asked me to come back later because her co-director wasn't there. By this time I was a bit pissed off, just wasn't used to that sort of treatment. But I came back, was asked to do more work, asked if I could sing, and finally she came down and spoke to me face to face. My first impression was of a dynamic figure, full of energy but still relaxed and easy

to speak to. I found it very difficult to keep up with her, she'd switch from subject to subject, refer to a gread fund of knowledge and assume that everybody knew as much as she did.

Finally I was hired. I walked into the theatre on a Monday morning, was confronted with a stunning set and told immediately to go up to wardrobe. I performed that same night. I was being directed at a level that I'd never met before, terms were used that were completely new to a standard rep actor. At the end of the show a character walked on stage and made an appeal to the audience for money – that was Gerry Raffles. He then introduced himself and me – the most wonderful character who seemed to love all human beings. We all went out for a Chinese meal by the docks, Gerry was the host who made sure that everybody had food and was enjoying the drink. Joan sat very quiet, the pattern was that in the theatre Gerry let Joan be the explosive one, outside of it Gerry was dominant. It was like being taken into a complete family.

In January 1954 Harry H. Corbett played the title role in *Richard II*. It was a successful production, was revived a year later, but probably suffered in comparison with an Old Vic rendering at the same period. The real breakthrough came in the summer of 1955 with *Arden of Faversham* which was the culmination of five years' work. Maxwell Shaw again:

Today the training for the play wouldn't seem particularly revolutionary, but in the early fifties it most certainly was. Joan believed then in presenting every play close to the style in which it was written, not to do built up versions. Voice classes, movement, attention to the period, access to the background of the time, listening to hours of sixteenth-century music and being lectured on the values of the time – all this was new to actors of the time. Today it's considered essential, fundamental.

Soon after came *The Good Soldier Schweik*, which was the first Stratford transfer to the West End. It was not particularly well-received at the Duke of York's although its popularity at the Theatre Royal had resulted in some of Workshop's most lucrative evenings of the first few years. *An Italian Straw Hat* and a well-reviewed *Edward The Second* followed, both playing to extremely good houses. Harry Corbett left the company at the end of 1955, leaving Avis Bunnage, Howard Goorney, Maxwell Shaw and Gerard Dynevor as the more experienced actors at Stratford.

One of the consistent policies of Joan Littlewood and Gerry Raffles was to read every script sent in to the theatre. Usually this was a fruitless exercise, but it could, occasionally, prove rewarding. At the beginning of 1956 an aspiring writer named Brendan Behan sent in a play called *The Quare Fellow* to Stratford after it had been turned down by the Abbey Theatre, Dublin. Born in 1923 in a Dublin slum, Behan had been expelled from school, had served time in borstal in 1939 for planning to blow up a Liverpool dock in the cause of the Irish Republican Army and in 1942 was sentenced to fourteen years' imprisonment by an Irish military court for attempted murder. He was released after the Second World War under a general amnesty, and was in a Manchester prison a year later. *The Quare Fellow* was based on Behan's experiences in jail and told of the last twenty-four hours in the life of a condemned man.

Joan Littlewood worked incessantly on Behan's witty and compassionate play, and, by the final rehearsal the scope, size and sheer power of the work had increased almost beyond recognition; on seeing the final version Behan confessed that 'Miss Littlewood's company had performed a better play than I wrote'. Brendan Behan met with considerable controversy and fame some years later with *The Hostage,* but the anecdotes from his earliest days at Stratford are legion. A favourite story of his was: 'Did I ever tell you about my old auntie who came to see a little funny play I wrote for a festival in Ireland? . . . Everybody laughed, seemed to love it. But my auntie coughed a lot and told them to shut up. At the end of the show she stood up and told them that they were "a lot of ignorant bastards for laughing at my nephew's beautiful play".'

On the first night of *The Quare Fellow* the audience included at least three IRA activists, two detectives and a score of republican supporters. Howard Goorney estimates that half the audience stood to attention when the Irish national anthem was sung during the play. The reviews were stunning; Behan was hailed as a new Irish genius discovered in a forgotten corner of London. The production transferred to the Comedy Theatre and went on to tour in Cambridge and Liverpool. Maxwell Shaw knew Behan intimately at the time.

He had a bigger personality even than Gerry and that's saying something. The two of them got on marvellously, very sympathetic to each other, and Gerry was drinking in those days. The food, the bonhomie, the jokes. And Joan adored Brendan. He had a character which was unusual, because someone who is such an extrovert and a storyteller doesn't usually care much for individuals. He did though, and like Gerry he always had time to talk to people one to one. He would praise a performance, tell you it reminded him of a relative or an incident.

He'd been involved in theatre before, but never with such a close-knit group. For Brendan it represented a family, and when he was with family he sang, drank and told jokes. So of course he would come round before the show and appear in the dressing room with a crate of Guinness, and with Brendan there was no refusing. Joan was appalled at this, quite appalled.

Behan's actions had more effect than he ever realized: his habit of engaging the cast in gentle conversation until only minutes before the beginning of a performance was to change the underlying style of Theatre Workshop. Since the move to Stratford both Littlewood and Raffles had been committed to the notion that a performance had to begin hours before the play started. They demanded that all members of the cast be in the theatre as much as two hours before the curtain went up, during which time the actors would think themselves into the life of their character, concentrating fully on the play and their part in it – the Stanislavsky ideal. It undoubtedly contributed to much of the success of the early productions.

On a tour of *Arden of Faversham* in France, however, this process was forcibly changed. On the evening of a performance to be given to an audience of dignitaries, the British ambassador arrived forty-five minutes late. During the wait European photographers appeared from behind the props to take intrusive pictures, all of the ritual character-concentration was forgotten and Littlewood paced the floor resigned to the fact that the performance would be a total disaster. It wasn't. In fact, it was given the best reviews that Theatre Workshop ever received.

What Joan Littlewood had failed to take into account was that a particular character becomes second nature to, and an integral part of, a good actor over a period of time. *Arden of Faversham* proved this, but one of Littlewood's faults was a marked reluctance to admit defeat. She rejected the implications of the 'Arden' incident, but as Brendan Behan continued making his excursions into dressing-rooms before the curtain went up, a certain informality took over and she accepted the new approach with little comment.

Nineteen fifty-seven saw an influx of fresh blood into the theatre. Among the most memorable and important of the new generation of young actors who had been encouraged to enter the profession was Murray Melvin. A former shipping clerk from Hampstead, he had gone to see *Edward The Second* and *Richard II* and shortly afterwards was offered a place and a grant to study at the Guildhall School of Music and Drama. He approached Gerry Raffles with the proposal that he work as a student, actor and assistant stage manager at Stratford with the grant as payment, and reject the coveted Guildhall place. Raffles agreed.

My first job as a student at the Theatre Royal [Melvin recalls] was to paint the front of the building. Within an hour of me getting up on to that ladder most of the people in the houses next to the theatre knew exactly what I was doing, where I came from and what I wanted to do. My second job was to paint the foyer. That was the introduction to my university, and university is what it was.

Shortly after *The Quare Fellow* Joan Littlewood took one of her periodic vacations from the theatre, leaving John Bury to produce several plays, including *The Playboy of the Western World* and *The Duchess of Malfi*. On her return she directed *Macbeth*, which later toured Moscow, and then *You Won't Always be on Top* – a play which had begun life as a fairly bland piece, and ended by being extremely controversial. Written by a building worker named Henry Chapman, it portrayed the lives of ordinary builders in a naturalistic manner. Theatre Workshop worked on it, making massive amendments and using improvisation, and it became a humorously cutting tirade against society. It was also helped by John Bury's set which necessitated the cast learning how to lay bricks and actually constructing a wall on stage. Two heavy and substantial pieces of scaffolding were used, and on one occasion a zealous Murray Melvin found, to his distress, that he had one foot on each and that the two structures were slowly dividing. Only the speedy intervention of John Bury saved him.

When it finally opened with Richard Harris in the leading role, *You Won't Always be on Top* in no way resembled the script which had been submitted to the Lord Chamberlain's office and Gerry Raffles, John Bury, Joan Littlewood, Henry Chapman and Richard Harris subsequently appeared in court. Supported by public sympathy and a favourable review from Kenneth Tynan, a fighting fund was established with George Devine, Peter Hall and Lord Lever all acting as sponsors. The defendants were found guilty, fined the derisory sun of £15 and the Theatre Royal added another triumph to its list.

In spite of the international artistic impact of the Theatre Royal in these years, it was still fighting for its very existence. In between performances and rehearsals the cast of *The Quare Fellow* or *Edward The Second* would clean floors, paint walls and repair doors. The theatre's ancient heating system was still turned on only thirty minutes before a performance in the winter, and hardened audiences knew to bring along rugs and hot-water bottles. By 1958, their grants and subsidies in total came to less than £2,000 and there had still not been a completely full house. But there was help to come.

After the first performance of John Osborne's *Look Back in Anger* at the Royal Court Theatre on 8 May 1956 the existing boundaries of dramatic theatre had been irreversibly extended. In the next few years writers came forward in large numbers to articulate their lives, express the views and feelings of a class which had hitherto been gagged. Many of them came to nothing, Brendan Behan was one exception, and Shelagh Delaney was another. Born and raised in the overpoweringly industrial Lancashire town of Salford in 1939, she failed her 11-plus, left school at sixteen and worked for a time in a factory. From the age of seventeen she worked on a play, the background and motivation for which was drawn from her own life and experiences. *A Taste of Honey* was about a poor mother and daughter, the relationship between that daughter and a black sailor, and later with a homosexual student, and the environment they lived in.

Although there is no doubting Shelagh Delaney's talent, the contribution of Littlewood and her company was vital. Joan Littlewood was later to write: *'Taste of Honey* I adapted and built up from dialogue sent to me by Shelagh Delaney, the love scenes alone being her original work untouched.' Avis Bunnage had been the victim of one of Littlewood's unprovoked bouts of indignation shortly before rehearsals for the play began. After being ostracized for three months she was tempted back to the theatre and was offered the role of the mother.

> We had to do all our own stage management, Murray Melvin even had to pull the curtains just before it was his turn to come on stage. A lot of the costumes were my own, we had no money and the run was supposed to last for two weeks.
>
> Before long there was gossip about a transfer, but that's always the way. Then we heard that somebody wanted to buy 'Honey' and put it into the West End with a completely new star cast, Joan, of course, was having none of that – they either took it with the people who'd created the parts, or not at all.

Murray Melvin had been with the theatre only for a short time and was still training when he was given the character of Geoffrey, a part which was to found his acting career.

> There were five people in it because they couldn't afford six, and one of the five was the ASM. At the beginning it was just another play, the only difference being that Joan usually liked to work with a lot of people — economics were against her, she couldn't this time.
>
> Where people go a little wrong is when they use the awful phrase 'Kitchen Sink Drama'. This wasn't the Royal Court, we didn't have a sink on stage and we mimed drinking and pouring tea, and eating biscuits. It was fantasy, Joan didn't do kitchen sink drama. We could tell, those on the stage, that something special was going on. There were of course very good audiences, (apart from the last week of the first run when there was a bus strike on) and

the reviews were extremely good. My character wasn't fully understood, they usually referred to him as 'waif-like' but when the second production was mounted they went screaming overboard for it. It was realized what an important step it had been in the historical context of theatre. Then of course we had a Lord Chamberlain, and when the film came along it was 'X' certificate — now, it's an O-level text.

The play eventually tranferred to the West End to play at Wyndham's and later at the Criterion. In the film version Murray Melvin continued in the role of Geoffrey but a young Rita Tushingham played Josephine and Dora Bryan played her mother. All the screen adaptations of Theatre Workshop productions have come in for severe criticism, particularly from Workshop members. Avis Bunnage complains: 'When you've been involved with the original you really can't stand to watch people delivering lines which *you* threw in in the first place. After she saw the film Joan said "My God, Dora Bryan says those words as if they were great literary products, we used to make them up".'

The success, both in Stratford and the West End and in the cinema, of *A Taste of Honey* aided the theatre financially, but money was still the most immediate problem. In June 1958 the Arts Council decided to withdraw its grant on the mystifying pretext that support from local councils and audiences was insufficient. The relationship between Joan Littlewood and the Arts Council, and for that matter authority in general, had been strained ever since Workshop had moved to Stratford. Some years later Philip Hedley, later to direct the theatre, had to prolong an Arts Council meeting until the evening while he argued the case for Theatre Workshop. The council had listed Littlewood's company along with several obscure groups asking for grants under the heading of 'New Projects'. Hedley eventually won the day, but was shocked at the council's prejudices.

Joan Littlewood did nothing to ease the situation. She lived by the maxim that it is the duty of artists to bite the hand that feeds them. On one occasion a local council meeting which was to consider raising the Theatre Royal's subsidy coincided with a demonstration outside the town hall by housewives angry over the poor state of education in the borough. Littlewood proceeded to join the protest, was interviewed and photographed by journalists, and only appeared in front of the men and women who were to consider her case half an hour later. The grant was not raised.

Gerry Raffles's attitude to bureaucracy was one of complete distrust. Since 1953 he had had to use every means at his disposal, often unconventional ones, to maintain the theatre. The constant use of several cheque-books, the procuring of loans and the sheer financial commitment of everybody involved, left local politicians incredulous. 'You cannot tell me', expostulated a councillor to a theatre administrator in the bar, 'that those two aren't making a fortune out of the borough'.

The 1958 incident provoked a heated debate in *The Times* between Littlewood and the Arts Council, and support for the theatre began to be raised. Graham Greene offered £100, asking nine others to join him, together providing the amount of the Arts Council's grant. In one of the programmes for *A Taste of Honey* an insert stated: 'Provided we are allowed by economic circumstances, by the goodwill of the landlord, and by a change of heart on the part of the Arts Council, we will reopen this theatre in the Autumn of 1958 with another series of new or forgotten plays which help to interpret the modern world in exciting dramatic terms.' On this occasion the local council raised its contribution, which had been very low considering the prestige which the Theatre Royal was bringing to a severely depressed borough, and the Arts Council accordingly revoked its decision. The theatre was to reopen after a closure of three months.

The play chosen to open the rest of the season was the long-awaited new work by Brendan Behan. Between the success of *The Quare Fellow* and the writing of *The Hostage* Behan's drinking had reached the first stages of a tragic problem. His friends had been forced to take absurd measures to make him write, including locking him in a room and refusing to provide any food until he delivered pages of manuscript. Like *A Taste of Honey, The Hostage* was in the end the result of collaboration and improvisation. Littlewood recalls that *The Hostage* 'was conceived by Brendan and myself – I built a play from his one act, translated from the Irish, rewrote it and constructed two more acts after discussion with him. He supplied the songs.'

Originally written for the Gaelic League, the work leans heavily on Behan's life in the Irish Republican Army. The plot concerns an eighteen-year-old boy who is sentenced to death after the killing of an Ulster policeman. The IRA take a British soldier as a hostage, hide him in a brothel, and will only release him if the Irish boy is freed. The denizens of the brothel befriend the soldier, until he is shot dead during a raid. The play aims to show the futility of sectarianism and the difficulties of living in modern Ireland. The production played to the first capacity audience of Theatre Workshop at Stratford East, and caused a euphoric Gerry Raffles to pace around the building shouting: 'There must be a bloody "House Full" sign somewhere!' He eventually found one hidden away in a corner underneath the stage.

Murray Melvin had been unemployed after his success in *A Taste of Honey* until Joan Littlewood called him back to Stratford to take the part of the British soldier in the new play. For him it remains the finest work ever performed at Stratford.

It was an extraordinary period. The IRA thought the play was going to be anti-IRA, and on the first night we were all terrified. Howard Goorney will bear that out, he was under the table on more than one occasion during rehearsals. The theatre was ringed by Scotland Yard, and the IRA had threatened to shoot us all. As was pointed out, if they did shoot the first person to go would be me, the British soldier. Nothing happened of course, one critic said that if the IRA were there they wouldn't have been able to shoot straight for laughing.

The Hostage was later revived at Stratford, was taken to the Sarah Bernhardt Theatre for the Paris Festival and ran at Wyndham's Theatre in Charing Cross Road. But the atmosphere and intensity of the early performances at Stratford were never properly recaptured. Kenneth Tynan, an ardent admirer and constructive critic of Workshop, enthused:

Some of the speech is brilliant mock-heroic; some of it is merely crude. Some of the songs are warmly ironic; others are more savagely funny. Some of the acting is sheer vaudeville; some of it (Murray Melvin as the captive, and Celia Salkeld as the country girl whom, briefly and abruptly, he loves) is tenderly realistic. The work ends in a mixed, happy jabber of styles, with a piano playing silent-screen music while the cockney is rescued and accidently shot by one of the lodgers, who defiantly cries, in the last line to be audibly uttered: 'I'm a secret policeman, and I don't care who knows it!'

Inchoate as it often is, this is a prophetic and joyously exciting evening. It seems to be Ireland's function, every twenty years or so, to provide a playwright who will kick English drama from the past into the present. Mr Behan may well fill the place vacated by Sean O'Casey. Perhaps more important, Miss Littlewood's production is a boisterous premonition of something we all want – a biting popular drama that does not depend on hit songs, star names, spa sophistication, or the more melodramatic aspects of homosexuality. Sean Kenny's setting, a skeleton stockade of a bedroom surrounded by a towering blind alley of slum windows, is, as often at this theatre, by far the best in London.

For the play's author only six years of life remained. Lionized in the United States and supplied with drink by unscrupulous journalists, Behan was never to fulfil his enormous potential. During early rehearsals for *The Hostage* he would sit down on the edge of the stage, share out a crate of Guinness and talk to the assembled actors in brilliant and articulate prose for hours on end. His descriptions of Irish characters, as all of the original cast agree, were the basis of the final acting performances. As alcohol took its inevitable toll, Behan's actions took on a note of pathos. At the beginning of the Stratford season of his play he would interrupt the drama to provide a new line or an extra song. The actors never felt comfortable about this, but Behan's humour saved the situation. When audiences came – or so it appeared – simply to see Brendan Behan on his feet, the great man would become more outrageous, and more drunk. He would mumble incoherently, and in place of sardonic interjections vapid songs would be delivered in an alcoholic haze. As a bribe to keep him out of the auditorium he was allowed to appear on the stage at the end of the performance. An Irish jig would be danced, the audience would cheer, and Behan would be laughing with, as well as at, the English. When the next production arrived, *A Christmas Carol,* Behan would still walk on stage at the end – once being mistaken by a child in the audience for Charles Dickens.

After *The Hostage* and Littlewood's popular version of the Dickens classic a contemporary musical by Frank Norman followed up the virtually unbroken success of Stratford. Norman had originally written the nucleus of *Fings Ain't Wot They Used t'be* in 1958 but had not persevered with it. Through a mutual acquaintance it came to Joan Littlewood, and was first performed on 17 February 1959. Set in a gambling club full of undesirables, it relied on Frank Norman's personal experience of prostitutes, razor thugs and Soho crime. Littlewood had been introduced to songwriter Lionel Bart shortly before this time, and was anxious that he should contribute a musical element to Norman's play. The result was successful, but the repercussions were problematic.

The informal structure of Theatre Workshop and the obsession with improvisation which Joan Littlewood had, and had fostered in her followers, was accepted by Brendan Behan and Shelagh Delaney. Frank Norman was not so enthusiastic. Littlewood claims that she was given twenty-eight pages of dialogue by Norman, and that she adapted and built it up. Over the years various commentators have queried the actual figure, but Norman is adamant that his first contribution was forty-eight pages. As well as feeling indignant at attacks made on him, Norman was unhappy at the way his ideas were transformed, stated that he hardly recognized the final version, and the argument has never been satisfactorily settled. Be that as it may, the show ran for months at Stratford, was revived and then played at the Garrick Theatre for over two years.

After 'Fings' came a production of Marston's *The Dutch Courtesan* and a revival of *The Hostage*. By now many of the old regulars of Workshop were in the West End and a new team of actors was introduced. Eileen Kennally, Alfred Lynch and Ann Beach joined for the new rendering of the Behan play. When Wolf Mankowitz's *Make Me an Offer* came to Stratford in October 1959 it was the signal for a completely new style of drama, performed by fresh actors and directed by a newly inspired Joan Littlewood. Mankowitz was a writer of sentimental novels and plays, and *Make Me an Offer* was considered his best work. It describes the evolution of a market trader into a less than honest antiques dealer. The production did well, and moved to the New Theatre in December. Like Norman, Mankowitz had not always been happy with the improvisation but the cast of Daniel Massey, Diana Copeland and the as yet little known Sheila Hancock made the most of what some viewed as a limited piece of literature.

The new approach to performance, design and direction was given the label 'Knees-up' by opponents as well as supporters. It was to sustain Stratford East for the rest of Littlewood's years at the theatre, and for some latecomers came to represent the total achievement of Theatre Workshop. Maxwell Shaw says of it:

> In *Make Me an Offer* Joan met actors from a very different background from those that she'd been used to in the past. Through Victor Spinetti she met people like Barbara Windsor and Toni Palmer, and found that there was a lot of sincerity and a great many good things about their attitude to theatre. Everyone did their own thing and a lot of fun was had by all. Audience participation was genuine and real, there was belief in what was being done. But I do think that the earlier work was greater in its artistic achievement on all levels.

Director Lindsay Anderson had more reservations about the new-look Theatre Workshop.

> It was important because it made a very great impact, but it was probably more limited than the reputation which it enjoyed at the time. The chief problem with the theatre was a kind of intellectual limitation; while much of what was produced was subversive, because of the knees-up quality of the style it could be seen just as a nostalgic variety show. The problem with Joan was that her belief in popular theatre often fought with the dissident element, so you got a strong traditional music-hall influence, and all that rather regrettable and banal comedy about 'ponces' and 'queers' and 'tarts' and all that stuff. It didn't carry very far.

In the following production, William Saroyan's *Sam, the Highest Jumper of them*

All the 'Knees-up' style was temporarily dropped. Saroyan was an American writer who had been greatly impressed by the work of Brendan Behan and had telephoned Gerry Raffles to tell him so. During the conversation Raffles, never one for reticence, asked if Saroyan himself would be willing to write something for Stratford. Saroyan consented. Murray Melvin was to play the simple bank employee who, motivated by inadequacy, devotes himself to being the world's highest jumper. The play, peopled with characters such as Wally Wailer and Daisy Dimple, was heavily influenced by the Absurd. Much of the dialogue was developed during rehearsals, and although there were certain qualities about the production, both critics and public failed to register their approval.

In May 1960 came *Ned Kelly* by James Clancy, with Harry Corbett playing the supposedly misunderstood Australian outlaw. Once again the theatre did not have a particular success on its hands. After appearing at the Paris Festival in June with Ben Jonson's *Every Man in His Humour* the company returned to London and after a brief run of the same play before Stratford audiences, began rehearsals of *Sparrers Can't Sing*. By Stephen Lewis, this vivacious tale of an East End community was short on sub-plot and significance but long on affection and charm. Lewis had been a bricklayer before turning to writing and acting, and was surprised at the success of his efforts. The play itself changed enormously before its opening night, and Murray Melvin — who was to appear in the film version as well — was cast only by chance.

'Sparrers' began just after the new Green Room was made ready for us. I remember Joan bringing us all in there for a read-through of the play — she was always very keen on having as many as possible at first, changing the characters around a great deal and giving actors the female roles and actresses the male parts. I laughed all the way through the read, and at the end she asked me if I'd liked it. I said I had, and Joan asked if I wanted to be in it. Of course I did, but there wasn't a part for me. So I began rehearsals playing a character who isn't even in the play, he's only referred to as a 'bloke with red boots'. In the end I had a major part, that of Knocker Jug.

Joan Littlewood left the theatre for a holiday after the success of *Sparrers Can't Sing* and John Bury, given control, asked Harry Corbett to bring in a play he particularly wanted to direct. The choice was Alun Owen's *Progress to the Park*, a convincing story of a Protestant–Catholic relationship in Liverpool. Billie Whitelaw starred in the production, which later transferred to the West End.

Marvin Kane had written *We're Just Not Practical* for television, but brought the play which was about a couple who try their luck as housekeepers to Stratford as a stage work. From the very first Kane objected to some of Joan

Littlewood's methods, and he was finally 'excluded' from rehearsals. After a poor reception he went so far as to offer audiences their ticket money back if they were dissatisfied. This option was never employed, and *We're Just Not Practical* died a natural, if painful, death.

James Goldman's *They Might be Giants* ran for a less unpleasant but equally unsuccessful four weeks. Goldman had written a comedy about a retired judge who believes he is Sherlock Holmes. Harry Corbett and Avis Bunnage played Holmes and Watson, but few were impressed. This period also saw the establishment of the E.15 Acting School, under Margaret Bury. Students from all over the world as well as from all over the borough came to be taught by the likes of Brian Murphy and Harry Corbett, and one of the early ideals behind the scenes was for a new generation of Workshop actors to be groomed by Joan Littlewood's earlier graduates. As with many causes she began to lose interest in the school as soon as it was established.

One of the young people who was attracted by the opportunity of learning under the sons and daughters of Joan Littlewood was Philip Hedley. He was to play an important part in the theatre's development before becoming Littlewood's assistant in the early seventies. He observed her, Gerry Raffles for her and the workings of Stratford at first hand:

> She had an aura, though I suspect that as you become older and more famous that becomes inevitable. She was spellbinding. Absolutely spellbinding. When she decided to give someone her full attention it was almost a process of entertainment. I remember her gesticulating wildly, leaning forward to me and saying 'You see, I found my life on the rock of change' and she would often talk in those contradictions, paradoxes, and usually make perfect sense. There's hardly an adjective you can think of that Joan wasn't. She was both the most generous person you could meet, and she could be the toughest. She loved conflict, enjoyed provoking and could demolish people – and then she'd go and make them a meal in the Green Room.
>
> On one glorious occasion she was talking to the fireman on stage during his inspection, and I heard him say 'I'm only doing my job'. I sat down and listened, knowing what was going to happen. She started in the 1600s about the inquisition, through history to the gas chambers, the Spanish civil war and so on. This poor man was only complaining, quite rightly, about some bricks which had been removed from the proscenium arch; she quoted day, time and place for ten minutes while she literally talked him out of the building. It was a stunning invective, she seemed able to recall facts and dates without effort.

She was giving notes before *The Hostage* in the Green Room, which must have lasted two hours, during which she turned to Patience Collier, said 'How old are you?' – which is not the sort of thing you said to Patience Collier. Patience gave her age. And Joan said 'You're that old, and you still said that line in that way!' She quoted Brecht at her, quoted Shaw, quoted the woman who lived over the road. Sometimes she would calculatedly provoke somebody, but she also attacked because she just took a dislike, you could never be entirely sure. Sudden flashes of charm, little notes which she'd spent hours on. And then you'd be cut dead.

Hedley also witnessed the relationship between Joan Littlewood and Gerry Raffles at close quarters.

They were in love of course. She could also use him as her Aunt Sally at times – if we were opening next week and she wasn't satisfied she'd point up to the circle, where he usually sat, and say 'It's all his fault'. He devoted his life to Theatre Workshop, and more particularly to her.

A lot of people would speak against Gerry because of the contractual things he's done to them, but that was his job, to take all of the business pressure from Joan, and because of that he did make enemies. He was a big, handsome man with a huge laugh. Very big presence. He'd worked at many things, in the mines at one time, and there's a story that he tried to bring his father's factory workers out on strike. Because of that power he wasn't in her shadow, although he was younger than her. Joan was always very keen to know what he thought. They had rows, the old hands were used to them, and whenever she attacked him he would just sit back and puff on his pipe.

After *They Might be Giants* Littlewood's attitude changed discernibly, she had lost much of her early enthusiasm. That production had acted as the proverbial last straw. Critics had come down in packs to view the work, Littlewood had had to work with them in mind and it was something she was simply not used to doing or willing to continue doing. Through Arts Council grants, donations from organizations and local authorities and general goodwill the theatre could now count on just over £6,000 annually – an insulting sum. Benefits from West End transfers had been of little help, and furthermore, the cream of the old company was now working away from Stratford. Those who remained began once again, to voice their justifiable dissatisfaction at being expected to live on £15 a week. Tired, less happy than she had been for a long time and anxious to cover new ground, in 1961 Joan Littlewood decided to leave Theatre Workshop and travel to Nigeria.

In a letter to *Encore* she explained her thoughts and motives:

Such a lot of nonsense has been talked about my reasons for leaving England that I wanted to write to you before I went. You have always given serious consideration to the problems facing people working in the English theatre.

It is not unusual for someone to leave a situation in which they cannot do the work for which they are qualified. That is my case.

My objective in life has not changed; it is to work with other artists — actors, writers, designers, composers — and in collaboration with them, and by means of argument, experiment and research, to help to keep the English theatre alive and contemporary.

I do not believe in the supremacy of the director, designer, actor or even of the writer. It is through collaboration that this knockabout art of theatre survives and kicks. It was true at The Globe, The Curtain, The Crown, and in the 'illustrious theatre' of Molière and it can work here, today.

No one mind or imagination can foresee what a play will become until all the physical and intellectual stimuli, which are crystallized in the poetry of the author, have been understood by a company, and then tried out in terms of mime, discussion and the precise music of grammar: words and movement allied and integrated. The smallest contact between characters in a remote corner of the stage must become objectively true and relevant. The actor must be freed from the necessity of making effective generalizations.

I could go on but you too know how the theatre must function if it is to reflect the genius of a people, in a complex day and age. Only a company of artists can do this. It is no use the critics proclaiming overnight the genius of the individual writer; these writers must graft in company with other artists if we are to get what we want and what our people need, a great theatre.

This does not depend on buildings, nor do we need even a fraction of the money they are spending on their bomb. Each community should have a theatre; the West End has plundered our talent and diluted our ideas; cannot each district afford to support a few artists who will give them back some entertainment, laughter and love of mankind?

Young actors and actresses, don't be puppets any longer! The directors and the critics won't help you; in television, film or theatre they ask for the dregs of the old acting, mere 'expression', exploitation of your 'type'. In Shaftesbury Avenue or in the Brecht theatre, it's all the same. The theatre should be made up of individuals, not pawns. Keep your wits, develop your talent, take over the theatre which now belongs to the managers or the landlords. Let's stop this waste of human ability. I have tried, for nearly

Make Me an Offer, 1959 – Victor Spinetti spins partner

16

Barbara Windsor and Victor Spinetti in
Fings Ain't Wot They Used t'be: 'Knees Up
epitomized

17

Theatre Workshop's 21st: Gerry Raffles is
the Joseph-like shirt surrounded by his
people at a party onstage

18

Pierrots and polemics: *Oh What a Lovely War*, 1963

Raffles with constant companion

Joan. Erratic, inspired and usually brilliant

The obvious is pointed out by Ken Hill. Few saw it for many years

Maxwell Shaw. What went wrong?

23

Clare Venables may have been the right person at the wrong time

twenty-seven years. I've had my nose to the grindstone and I'm still, comparatively speaking, alive. I'll be back, I'll be more help.

When Theatre Workshop was not performing and the theatre was not dark there was a short season of plays backed by Oscar Lowenstein and produced on a day-to-day basis by Michael White. *The Secret of the World* by Ted Allan with Miriam Karlin and John Bury ran quite successfully and an Irish flavour was introduced into the proceedings by director Alan Simpson who worked on some productions and by an all-Irish musical. But there was never any intention, or possibility, of replacing Joan Littlewood and her company and however much she may have protested that she was finished with Stratford East, a sense of the inevitability of Littlewood's return remained in most people's minds. Echoes of Workshop were heard in January 1963 when Brian Murphy produced *High Street, China* by Robin Chapman and Richard Kane. The play about a day in the life of a boxer, ran for over six weeks; and was followed by *Oh What a Lovely War*.

It took a project on the grand scale – an exposure of the callousness, stupidity and heroism of the First World War – to bring a new Theatre Workshop and a refreshed Joan Littlewood back to Stratford. The idea had been sparked off by a radio show constructed by Charles Chilton around well-known songs of 1914 to 1918 – though members of the original cast of *Oh What a Lovely War* are at pains to stress that Chilton's involvement went no further. Littlewood had conceived the idea of investigating the events and characters of the war and then transmitting them on to the stage through a series of musical chapters. Instead of the actors dressing in the dull uniforms of the British Tommy, they would wear the costumes of a pierrot troupe and be known as 'The Merry Roosters'.

The company was assembled and each member was given an aspect of the war to research. After reading and studying the use of gas, the battle of Ypres, the Somme or the visit of the King they would report back and be questioned. It was these discussion groups which gave birth to the play. The experience was a moving one. A ritual came about whereby at 11.30 in the morning Gerry Raffles would bring a tray of drinks into the Green Room or on to the stage, and a shaken, sometimes tearful, cast would have to rest before they could throw themselves back into the horrors of the 'war to end all wars'.

In 1963 the real facts of the war were only just beginning to emerge because of the fifty-year rule on official secrets. British propaganda had clouded the issue, shrouding it in glory, for half a century. A.J.P. Taylor's history of the war, a crucial text, was published in 1963. It was a cutting analysis of what really happened during four years of battle. It was also dedicated to Joan Littlewood. And Murray Melvin, who also appeared in the play in Paris and New York, was forced to leave his agent because of what was seen as a vicious attack on the officer class of the British Army.

The form of *Oh What a Lovely War* was shaped by two now familiar but then as yet virtually untried techniques: a large screen was placed behind the actors showing photographs of the period and lists of casualties; and the idiom of the working-class soldier, the unpretentious song, was used to convey the thoughts and hopes of those whose war it really was. There was however, a certain naïveté about the production: the source of all evil was traced to the gentlemen and officers who ruled society and the private and corporal were without sin. The play's effect was stunning. Murray Melvin played one of the pierrots.

The time was right. Any earlier and those who had lost people would still have been grieving. We knew we were on dangerous ground, that was where we wanted to be. When we took it to France, Gaullism was in the air and we went so far as to prepare exits from the stage in case of a riot. There was no need: the audience stood up and cheered.

By the time we got to New York the Vietnam war had begun and victory fever had set in. People walked out in groups during the show. I remember those marvellous Quakers who kept up a twenty-four hour vigil in Times Square against the war. They were beaten, spat upon and abused. We gave them free tickets, and they'd come back at the end to our dressing-rooms with tears in their eyes, thanking us for coming to America. Some in Britain said we were dancing on dead men's graves, and that hurt so much. But we didn't take curtain calls, we walked off stage and left a photograph of the boys in the trenches waving and smiling – theirs was the applause. And if we did attack those bloody lieutenants, they were meant to be leaders of men so what the hell were they doing leading them to their graves? The whole point was to make war ugly. If ever a scene came over as being too attractive Joan would make us start again. 'No', she'd shout, 'you'll have them joining up'.

Avis Bunnage missed the early stages of *Oh What a Lovely War* due to filming commitments. She resisted the requests of Gerry Raffles for her to join the cast at first, but incessant phone calls and a more than persuasive Joan Littlewood eventually convinced her.

I took Ann Beach's part after a few weeks, with the intention of standing in for a short spell. After the first night I went to say goodbye to Gerry and he'd organized me to play for a full season without even asking me. I personally wasn't conscious of the impact we were making in wider terms; we'd see people walking out, and I remember at the end of one matinee a man crying his heart out, but that was the effect of the songs on the individual.

Victor Spinetti was to receive outstanding notices for his performance in the production. He had first joined Theatre Workshop in 1959 to play in *Make Me an Offer* and met Joan Littlewood on the stage of Wyndham's Theatre shortly before the West End run of *The Hostage* She introduced herself and asked Spinetti what he would give her for the set. 'About a quid,' he answered. She informed him that it had been acclaimed by everybody who had seen it. 'All right, ten bob then,' was the second answer. In the next couple of minutes the following dialogue ensued:

Joan: How would you like to play Charlie in this play?
Spinetti: OK.
Voice from the stalls: Darling, Charlie is the lead.
Joan: Right, you're playing the fucking lead.

A friendship between the two blossomed, with Joan going to see Spinetti in a strip club completing a season he had undertaken before going to Stratford. His memories of *Oh What a Lovely War* are particularly poignant:

Whether there is anything in reincarnation I don't know; I do know that since I was a boy I'd reacted in a frightening way to the First War and anything connected with it. As a schoolboy in Wales I was physically sick when the headmaster's car came in covered with poppies. I loathed the songs of the time, hated all that masochistic thumbs-up stuff and the 'it'll be all right' mentality. So when we all sat round and Joan played us the music I told her I hated it. 'That's not a problem,' she said, 'you can play the MC.' I did.

Official protests were made about the content. The War Office wrote to the theatre complaining about the statement that 100,000 men had been killed to capture ten yards of territory. Their letter said that in fact 100,000 'officers' and men were killed in the incident. Littlewood replied: 'We gave your officers the honour of calling them men.' Protests from the family of General Haig almost prevented a transfer to Wyndham's Theatre; one of the influences against this censorship came from an unlikely quarter, Princess Margaret. She had shown an interest in Stratford for some time, and went along to see *Oh What a Lovely War* with the Lord Chamberlain. Knowing that a member of the royal family would be in the audience, the cast toughened up some of the scenes. At the end of the performance the Princess said that much of what had been expressed should have been said a long time ago. She then turned to the Lord Chamberlain and asked if he agreed. He nodded enthusiastically. By June the play was in the West End.

The film of the stage success featured an all-star cast, was directed by Richard Attenborough and generally received bitter reviews. The same could not be said about the Stratford East rendering. Bernard Levin was enthusiastic in the *Daily Mail*:

> She's back! For far too long Miss Joan Littlewood, the Mother Courage of Theatre Workshop, has been away from home.
>
> At last, surrounded by a fine Theatre Workshop cast (it includes Murray Melvin, Brian Murphy, Griffith Davies and Victor Spinetti), she has returned in triumph with her first production for more than three years.
>
> The entertainment is stamped firmly with her trade-marks. It is a devastating musical satire on World War I, with the carnage played out amid the merry songs of the day ('We don't want to lose you, but we think you ought to go' may stand as an archetype), with a running band of lights upstage spelling out the casualties: 'Passchendaele: British loss 135,000 in the first day. Gain: 100 yards.'
>
> The result is, of course lopsided. (Miss Littlewood's faults are as much in evidence as her virtues.) The war was only fought because of the profiteers and only the other ranks were any good. (She would do well to remember that Wilfred Owen and Siegfried Sassoon were both officers.)
>
> Still, the point about such lopsidedness about World War I is that the lop is on the right side.
>
> The villain of the piece, for instance, squarely and without reservations, is Haig. We are not allowed to forget that for a Haig there was a Ludendorff and for both a Pétain: but it is on Haig that the author's sights, and Miss Littlewood's, are set, and right in the middle they get him, yapping eternally about the one big push that will see the Army through the enemy line, as the casualties mount from the thousands to the hundreds of thousands and the hundreds of thousands to the millions. 'Battle of the Somme: British loss 65,000 in three hours. Gain nil.'
>
> It is not as grim as that, in truth, Miss Littlewood's touch is light, and the humour is uppermost, even in the savage parody of a field service, with the men singing, to the tune of 'Onward, Christian Soldiers',
>
> > Forward, Joe Soap's Army,
> > Forward without fear,

With our brave commanders
Safely in the rear.

But be not deceived: even in the safe purlieus of Theatre Workshop, there were uneasy stirrings in the house at some of the things that were being done with the Union Jack, and when the inevitable transfer to the West End takes place, this may well be the first satire to score what we are told is the satirists's bull's eye: to make the audiences walk out.

In the following March, Frank Norman brought another work, *A Kayf up West,* to Stratford. Once again relying on his knowledge of the low life of Soho and its environs, Norman wrote about youth losing its innocence in the company of café society. Many in the thirteen-strong cast were new to Workshop methods and found it difficult to cope with constant doubling up of parts and the erratic demands of a director with a mission. The show was not a resounding success. The combination of critical attacks on *A Kayf up West,* yet more financial problems — total subsidies to the theatre at the time came to a mere £6,500 — and Joan Littlewood having only returned to Stratford under pressure caused another break-up of the company.

The group which came to Stratford East to replace Workshop was an ambitious team working under the title 'Stage Sixty'. Two experienced men were in charge, Adrian Rendle and David Thompson. Rendle had been director of the Tower Theatre for six years in the late fifties and had also produced in Northern Ireland. Thompson had gained his experience in the Oxford University Dramatic Society, had worked for the BBC and been art critic of *The Times.* Their stated aim was to build a company which was 'as independent and individual' as Theatre Workshop and to employ artists from other media as well as the theatre. In fact they were responsible for very few memorable evenings, and left substantial debts to their successors in 1967.

Workshop utilized their time away from Stratford by taking *Oh What a Lovely War* to the United States and appearing at the Edinburgh Festival with a production of Shakespeare's *Henry IV* (parts *I* and *II*). Heavily adapted and using both modern and Jacobean dress, it was not well received by the press but, as happened frequently in Stratford's history, was extremely popular with those who actually paid for their tickets. Joan Littlewood also spent some time in Tunisia where, along with other eminent directors from Britain, she initiated foreign students into the modern techniques of European theatre. Her other two interests at the time were not as rewarding. After achieving little besides bad feeling with Lionel Bart's musical *Twang* she began her obsession with what she termed the 'Fun Palace'. This forlorn hope was largely the product of her

49

disillusionment with British theatre. Something of a cross between the Pompidou Centre and an East End travelling funfair, the idea received the backing of Lord Harewood and Yehudi Menuhin as trustees. Possible sites included the Lea Valley, a spot by the Thames in central London and the forecourt area of a train or underground station.

The publicity blurb for the proposal had an intriguing appeal:

Arrive and leave by train, bus, monorail, hovercraft, car, tube or foot at any time. The information screens will show you what's happening. No need to look for an entrance — just walk anywhere. No doors, foyers, queues or commissionaires: it's up to you how you use it. Look around — take a lift, a ramp, an escalator to wherever or whatever looks interesting.

Choose what you want to do — or watch someone else doing it. Learn how to handle tools, paint, babies, machinery, or just listen to your favourite tune. Dance, talk or be lifted up to where you can see how other people make things work. Sit out over space with a drink and tune in to what's happening elsewhere in the city. Try starting a riot or beginning a painting — or just lie back and stare at the sky.

What time is it? Any time of day or night, winter or summer — it really doesn't matter. If it's too wet that roof will stop the rain but not the light. The artificial cloud will keep you cool or make rainbows for you. Your feet will be warm as you watch the stars — the atmosphere clear as you join in the chorus. Why not have your favourite meal high up where you can watch the thunderstorm?

Why all this lot? 'If any nation is to be lost or saved by the character of its great cities, our own is that nation.' Robert Vaughan 1843. We are building a short-term plaything in whch all of us can realize the possibilities and delights that a twentieth-century city environment owes us. It must last no longer than we need it.

Littlewood's Fun Palace project came to nothing and she returned to Stratford to prepare a production of Barbera Garson's *MacBird*. By this time new, younger people who had begun as adoring fans of Theatre Workshop were playing a part in moulding the final phase of their idol's existence. Peter Rankin first came to Stratford, playing truant when he was a teenager at Westminster School. He was told that he could watch rehearsals and be involved on the periphery of the theatre if he remained 'invisible'. He went on to act and direct, and his North London home is now Joan Littlewood's base when she visits London.

When I met her and told her that I was mad keen about the theatre she said it was absolutely terrible, I should be science-struck but not stage-struck. She let me help though, could be encouraging and marvellous and very unfair. She told me to get off the stage once, compared me to a cabbage, said that one of my movements in a play was like watching a turd on a blanket. Gerry was much more shy, claimed to have come into the theatre via politics. And their relationship was a tempestuous one. They were very much in love, but Joan refused to marry because she said he would find a girl who was much more pretty and much more fun. I don't think she ever meant it.

MacBird was a relentless satire on presidents Kennedy and Johnson and all they represented and was banned by the Lord Chamberlain from any public performance. The method used to get round this archaic ruling was to turn the Theatre Royal into a club, thereby eliminating the problem of the public performance. The notice for the production stated:

Banned. The Lord Chamberlain would not allow this play to be performed publicly, as he has to 'protect the heads of friendly states'. He was informed that it had been running in the US for some time. His reaction: 'Well, when it has been running longer in New York, without provoking protest, then maybe it could be shown here.'

So, you haven't seen *MacBird* advertised. You are missing theatre as it should be: caricature − yes, formality − no. This is not the sophisticated acting of worn-out cliché, but the spontaneous enthusiastic portrayal of an outrageous *version* of Kennedy's assassination, Vietnam and the pox Americana.

Because of the Lord Chamberlain's decision, you have to be a member of the Theatre Royal Club. LSE Union has affiliated *en masse*. Just show your LSE identification at the door, and you will be treated as a member of the club. This is more than just seeing a play − it is a laughing, fresh, nothing-sacred look at present day US politics − and if you are interested in Theatre Workshop, we would like to know what you think. Do let us know.

The same year saw the formation of Activists For Theatre Royal, Stratford, E15, a dedicated group of mostly young people passionately concerned with the theatre in general, and Stratford in particular. At an initial meeting in May they listed their objectives as: 'to make, in any and all ways possible, Theatre Royal, Stratford, E15 known to the 8,000,000 (?) inhabitants of London and its environs . . . to know what in return the public want from a "theatre".' Two leading lights on the committee decided to implement the first of these objectives by painting tiger's feet on the pavement from Stratford Broadway to the theatre. Within a week Joan Littlewood was writing to her solicitors on their behalf for help on a charge of breaking Section 117(1) of the Highways Act 1959 as amended by Section 7 of the Highways (Miscellaneous Provisions) Act, 1961.

But support for Stratford East from devoted followers did have more serious and rewarding repercussions. Nickolas Grace, who lived in nearby Woodford, was inspired by the work of Joan Littlewood and the theatre to become an actor. When he offered his services he was given the task of selling programmes, and has memories of 'Joan Littlewood wearing incongruous hats, Gerry Raffles telling me I couldn't work at Stratford because I was "too posh" and an overriding sense of friendliness and talent.'

The production that followed *MacBird* was *Intrigues and Amours*, based on Vanbrugh's *The Provok'd Wife*. It was drastically undercast, and precious rehearsal time was spent boning up on fundamental techniques and the basics of Restoration comedy. Littlewood was adamant that her company should approach the language of the late seventeenth century as if it were a stream: sticks and rocks could be dropped in periodically but the flow had to continue. Despite positive direction the thinness of the cast showed all too clearly.

Joan Littlewood did not spend all her time at Stratford concerning herself with the theatre. In 1967 she busied herself with the Children's Playground Project. On a site just outside the theatre, which was mostly rubble, she planned to build and develop a centre for local children, seeing the sad little plot of land as the last remaining outpost of the old Stratford. She was partially correct. In the next six years Stratford was to be transformed from a poor but vivacious town into a mass of concrete slabs; the theatre became a Victorian oasis in the middle of modern urban ugliness. Although Gerry Raffles managed to gain Listed Building status for the Theatre Royal there were constant attempts by developers to have it demolished. When Angel Lane was being violated Raffles was forced to tear down the barriers and wire which builders had erected next to the theatre; dust would seep into the shaking structure of the theatre as nearby houses were smashed, but the developers never had the chance to push a bulldozer even 'accidentally' through a supporting wall of Stratford East.

As with so many of Littlewood's later ideas, the playground ended in disappointment; there was no money to support the proposal. Both *MacBird* and *Intrigues and Amours* had been financial disasters – so much so that Raffles, who had always been strongly against the second, refused even to include them in official biographies – and the remaining members of the company were forced to busk in the local pub, The Red Lion, with Peter Rankin passing round the hat. Littlewood and a force of volunteers cleared the site of tin cans, bottles, rocks and rotting mattresses on a Sunday afternoon and then set about writing to 'sympathetic' firms for donations. Terence Conran of Habitat sent a package of broken toys.

For the first time, those inside the theatre got to know the children of the area. Rough as they were, when let loose on the playground and then on the stage of Stratford East they spontaneously created a drama based on their own lives. They regularly attended the theatre, were completely won over by Joan Littlewood and took to improvisation with relish. In an area which has one of the highest juvenile robbery rates in the country, Theatre Workshop kept children off the streets and gave them constructive opportunities. A film about the playground and its denizens was planned, but was never made. The children's interest declined, another theatre season started, and before long the Playground-Project was a thing of the past.

By September, sufficient money and enthusiasm had been raised to begin rehearsals on *Mrs Wilson's Diary*. Originally a feature in *Private Eye* magazine written by John Wells and Richard Ingrams, it had attracted a cult following by parodying the activities of Prime Minister Harold Wilson and his Labour Cabinet through the eyes of Mrs Wilson. With songs by Wells and a musical score composed by Jeremy Taylor the production was a surprising success, for in the early stages few people felt any excitment about it. Wells and Ingrams had read their version of the play to Joan Littlewood and her company in standard Oxbridge satirical voices, and the assembled actors had expressed their disapproval by ostentatiously passing around wrapped toffees. By the time the play was cast, matters had greatly improved, and Littlewood had managed to introduce substance and movement into what she had felt was a rather static text.

Richard Ingrams dropped out of the production but John Wells continued his involvement, and became committed to Stratford East. 'I was very impressed with how Joan had remained faithful to what we had written but had made it work on stage,' he explained. 'It looked just as Richard and I had imagined when we wrote it down.' With a cast of just eight it was the only show performed by Theatre Workshop to be financially successful on a large scale: and instead of being a fill-in piece with dubious support, it immediately transferred to the Criterion Theatre where it ran for nine months.

The last production of the season was Daniel Farson and Harry Moore's *The Marie Lloyd Story* which opened in November 1967 with Avis Bunnage in the title role. A moving and unapologetically show-business-based rendering of a tragic story, it told of the often lonely years of the famous music-hall star. With the performance of a lifetime from Avis Bunnage it was greeted with almost universal praise.

But the technical side of the production was not always to be counted on. During a preview, the main baton weight inside the stage curtain which lowered at the end of the performance landed with some force on Avis Bunnage's head. As the cast waited anxiously Joan Littlewood went up to her dressing-room to find out how bad the injury was. She was shaken but did not need to be taken to hospital. The opening night was postponed for three days and Tom Driberg decided to increase publicity for the show by writing that Bunnage had in fact been knocked unconscious. When she heard of the article a never less than candid Avis Bunnage exclaimed: 'Knocked out? I was called for bloody rehearsals first thing the following morning.'

The fact that the show did not transfer to the West End was largely due to the Brechtian songs included in the Stratford production. The administrators of the central London theatres wanted them to be cut; the composers would not have it. Even if the transfer had gone ahead it is doubtful that it could have prevented another leave of absence on the part of Littlewood and her company. They were replaced by a series of drag and variety acts, most of whom were not at all popular with a puritanical East London audience which expected better.

The next Workshop production those audiences were to see was directly connected with their lives and problems. Local govenment and the corruption therein had long been discussed as a subject for a drama. Ken Hill, who had worked for the Birmingham authorities, decided to take the idea further. In *Forward up Your End,* with a cartoon setting by Larry of *Punch* and music by Len Newberry, the banalities and dishonesty of provincial government were paraded for all to see. The humour, much to the disappointment of those involved, made more impact than the political content.

Forward up Your End was Ken Hill's first production at Stratford – he had been employed in a factory only two years before. As a writer he was to work on countless television scripts and took over the running of the Theatre Royal on Joan Littlewood's departure.

Everyone was in awe of Joan at first, but there's that thing about familiarity, isn't there? She taught me more than everyone else put together in theatre. The best. Truthfully. There are directors in the world who don't even know how much they owe to her. She was a great games player, any good director has to be. And because of that people's feelings did get hurt. She was terribly intolerant, terribly intolerant.

54

The other thing is that you must never separate Joan and Gerry when you talk of Theatre Workshop. Perhaps in the very early formative days it was only Joan, but by the time I joined, about 1970, Gerry was an integral part. They were responsible for developing Workshop, and development is an important factor. It didn't stand still, it changed. In 1970 the emphasis was on form, competence, art. If I understood it correctly, she was trying to make theatre totally and completely accessible, to make it a people's art form. That didn't mean she did mindless work. She believed that accessibility began when people came out of Stratford station, so they'd be met and greeted: people were made to feel that the theatre was as much theirs as anybody else's. Barriers were broken down, but accusations were and are made that some productions were facile.

The local government theme had been explored by Ken Hill, but with Stratford being at the centre of what could easily have been a 'how not to do it' example to aspiring councillors and planners, it was correctly assumed that targets nearer home should be attacked. In 1968 a hideous tower block known as Ronan Point had begun to collapse. The flats in question were to plague the Newham authorities for some sixteen years and in 1970 the story was still topical. Littlewood attended the trials which took place after the tower had crumbled and took copious notes with a view to using them as the basis for a play. She was told, however, that even if they were used verbatim it would be illegal, and thus would never be permitted. Her solution was to ask John Wells to find an alternative method of parodying the events and characters surrounding Ronan Point.

Wells decided to write a play in the eighteenth-century style and attribute it to a bogus playwright of the period named Rufus Chetwood. It was titled *The Projector* and managed to convince audiences and critics alike (until Alan Brien, taken into Wells's confidence, later told the truth of the matter in print). As cynics expressed their opinion, those at the theatre embellished the story. Chetwood had been a stage door-keeper at Drury Lane in the 1730s, the work had first been produced in 1733 and a copy of it was taken to America by one Emil Potbohm. John Wells recalls:

It all went surprisingly well. We had an eighteenth-century breakfast before the opening night, Carl Davis who wrote the music was dressed in period costume and played the harp at the front of the stage. Lord Aimwell, a character in it who hung around building sites waiting for young men, was based on Tom Driberg (he came to see it twenty-three times). There were some quite emotional bits, when a bunch of transvestites was hanged for example, and there were also a lot of problems with the farting sergeant – we couldn't get him to fart properly. It was very well researched, very atmospheric and really very successful.

Joan Littlewood's problems with the local council and other financing bodies continued into the 1970s. The theatre itself was threatened by the Newham authorities – Bill Tidy drew a cartoon entitled 'St Joan' in which Littlewood was tied to a stake and a character with 'Newham Council Official' on his back poured petrol on to the pyre – and after another show of hostility on the part of the Arts Council, the lights went out at Stratford East once again. When, however, in 1972 a grant of £40,000 was offered by the Arts Council, with another £20,000 from elsewhere, the production chosen to reopen the theatre was *The Londoners*. This was a musically adapted version of Stephen Lewis's *Sparrers Can't Sing* with Lionel Bart returning to Stratford to take charge of the score. Rita Webb was brought into the show, found it impossible to cope with the laxity which the rest of the Workshop-trained cast adopted as a matter of course, and walked out of the production every other day. But *The Londoners* managed to run for longer than its prearranged time and almost joined many predecessors with a transfer to the West End.

Brendan Behan had died in 1964 and a revival of one of his plays at Stratford was long overdue. The choice was *The Hostage,* and a trip was made to Ireland to recruit an authentic cast. By 1972 the IRA was much more than a memory, and what had been a romp became a cold work of drama set inside the Irish troubles. James Booth played the IRA man, with a Belfast accent, and one of the consequences was a spate of bomb scares which forced two complete evacuations of the building. American producer Ray Stark showed considerable interest in turning the play into a film, and the set at Stratford was designed with this in mind. After much procrastination Stark walked into the auditorium and said, without any explanation: 'Well, I've been talking to Princess Margaret and she doesn't think it's a great idea.' No more was heard.

Henry Irving's *The Ffinest Ffamily in the Land* was the next production at Stratford, running from the third week in July to the end of September. Maxwell Shaw and Brian Murphy starred in it. After returning from a holiday abroad Littlewood and Raffles decided to tackle the subject of package tours as material for a play. Only hours after landing in Britain they approached a surprised Frank Norman and Lionel Bart with the idea, and such was their confidence that posters were printed proclaiming that Norman and Bart were back together again. *Costa Packet* started life as a nine-page synopsis written by

Norman – Bart had only suggested a sub-title – and the verdict of the company was that half of it had great potential, the other half being without hope. Norman went off to work on his script, wrote a fuller play but managed to enlarge only on the half hated by the cast. Alan Klein was brought in and set about rewriting the text and composing the songs. Bart contributed two of his own.

The period of *Costa Packet* was an unhappy one for all concerned, and on the first night there was extreme reluctance even to take curtain calls or go to the bar to talk with the audience after the performance. The notices which came out the following morning were first class, a comic musical of the highest order had been seen. For ten weeks groups of ex-holiday makers and people with mass bookings from tour organizations laughed their way through what was seen by those involved as at best a competent piece.

The period after the 1972 Christmas was covered by *Big Rock Candy Mountain* by Alan Lomax, in which old Woody Guthrie and country songs were woven into a play. Peter Rankin recalls a special schools matinee performance: 'Five minutes before it was due to start there were only two rows of mongoloid children in the audience; apparently the schools hadn't got their grant and couldn't come. We performed anyway, and somehow those kids seemed to love every minute. We were all very moved.'

Ken Hill had emerged as one of the leading lights of the new Theatre Workshop in the early seventies, and in February 1973 his *Is Your Doctor Really Necessary?*, with its scathing attacks on the medical world and the drugs market, was produced. It was the first work Hill had actually directed at Stratford and its success ensured at least a short-term future for the theatre. One of the major successes of the show was the music by Tony Macaulay, who later wrote the hit musical *Windy City*. Ken Hill's spell of directing was followed by Maxwell Shaw working on C.G. Bond's *Sweeney Todd*, which in turn inspired Stephen Sondheim's musical at Drury Lane. Shaw had never been the most radical of the Workshop team, and this production relied less on improvisation than almost any play ever put on at Stratford.

In the summer of 1973 Joan Littlewood proposed an idea for a new development of Theatre Workshop which was to represent the final inspiration of the woman who had dominated British theatre for a decade. For some time writers and performers had met at Stratford to discuss new forms and occasionally take part in semi-serious revues. Littlewood had not been challenged by her work in any serious way since *Oh What a Lovely War*, and she decided to take the revue idea further, combining it with other non-mainstream theatre approaches. Her plan was for a season of shows called *Nuts*, consisting of a stream of sketches performed by an eight- or nine-strong body of actors, backed up by news items and gossip from journalists who would be invited to phone in information or come to Stratford themselves, and show business guests who would sing, act or recount anecdotes.

The structure of the show was to remain fairly static but the content was to change nightly. Often the result was a shambles, but the spontaneity and sheer excitement of the event impressed many who had begun to lose faith in Workshop. The installation of a large television screen on stage terrified some of the actors involved; its potential, however, was dramatic. Sometimes the varying aspects of the enterprise came together: one evening Myvanwy Jenn, recently back from the United States, sang a piece from *The Merry Widow* dressed in an all-white Edwardian costume, and the audience's response was tumultuous. As she finished a man jumped from the front row of the stalls, climbed on to the stage and proceeded to explain why he had become a communist. The extraordinary contrast worked, and Joan Littlewood approved heartily.

In November 1973 Joan Littlewood directed her last play at Stratford, Peter Rankin's *So You Want to be in Pictures.* It had been a short piece set on a film set in Rome, and forced padding did it no justice at all. After the production Littlewood finally left the Theatre Royal. For over a year she had been treating old supporters and friends in a manner which was less than reasonable. Actors who had been with her for years would phone asking for work, and often their calls would be ignored. They would then find that an untrained newcomer had been given a part. The theatre was being run on anarchic and immature lines, and Stratford as an area no longer held any joys for Joan Littlewood. But even though she had left the theatre, her influence was as strong as ever, and it is probable that she intended to visit frequently and even to direct again.

For the holiday period Philip Hedley came in to direct *A Christmas Carol* and the following February Ken Hill, now being groomed by Gerry Raffles to take over the management of the theatre, presided over a production of his *Gentlemen Prefer Anything.* Other plays followed but there was no sense of direction and the feeling was one of a disorganized interregnum. The financial situation was again precarious, and it is ironic that the fall of the Conservative government in 1974 and the end of the enlightened time in office of Arts Minister Norman St John Stevas worsened the theatre's fate. After further confrontations with the Arts Council, Gerry Raffles, never comfortable at Stratford without Littlewood, resigned and officially handed over the reins of power to an inexperienced Ken Hill.

Hill started his term with the concept of 'Adventure plays', believing that as someone brought up with the cinema he could adapt film action to the stage. To a large extent he was proved right, and was making considerable progress at the theatre with the approval of Littlewood and Raffles. Then, on 11 April 1975, at the age of fifty-one, Gerry Raffles died. He had suffered from diabetes and a heart complaint for some time, and while on holiday in the French town of Vienne the pressure of the two finally took its toll.

Joan Littlewood was beyond consolation. She heard the news of his death over the phone, and subsequently could not use a telephone for weeks. Her reaction to the death of her friend, companion and lover was comparable to that of Queen Victoria to the loss of her husband; but whereas the monarch blamed her son, Joan Littlewood held the theatre responsible. Her reactions have oscillated between wanting the building to be razed to the ground, and seeing it as a shrine to the man and his work. Indeed, the address of the theatre is now 'Gerry Raffles Square, E15.'

The impact of Raffles's death on those at the theatre was great. As father figure, best friend and adviser his solidity and good sense had been a driving force at Stratford for a generation. Littlewood vowed never to return to the theatre, nor has she, nor is she ever likely to. Her memory and influence continues, though, much of the time in the form of a proud past and an encouragement to strive for theatrical excellence; it can also act, however, as a dead weight around the neck of any director at Stratford.

To arrive at a balanced sober view of the influence and importance of Theatre Workshop would be only marginally less difficult than forcing Joan Littlewood to sit through hours of conventional drama at a plush Shaftesbury Avenue Theatre. By its very nature Workshop produced loyalty and antipathy; and because it happened a decade and more ago romance and complacency have had time to take hold. Neither are of much use to this book.

For those who acted and developed under Littlewood's guidance, theatre will never be the same, and never be as good. Their paths have been varied. While some have gone on to build substantial and lucrative careers in other parts of show business — some more lucrative than substantial — there is a core of Workshop graduates who have never quite fulfilled their heralded potential: a generation of actors in search of a director and a theatre.

Victor Spinetti remembers Workshop with affection:

Look Back in Anger was still a traditional play in form, that could never be said about most of the work we did. Joan held us extremely tightly, but inside you felt completely free. When you worked for her it wasn't for one season, it was for a lifetime. And yes, some of us have never been able to cope with the wider world. That doesn't diminish her influence. She liberated theatre, showed television the way and opened up new doors to new people. Olivier once said to me: 'I wish I could work in that way, but I'm a trained parrot.'

Guardian drama critic Michael Billington reviewed as many disappointments as successes at the Stratford of Raffles and Littlewood. He notes her influence on actors, but doubts its value in altering the ways of directors.

So many actors, Harry Corbett and Roy Kinnear for example, took what they learned at the Theatre Royal and loosened up English acting. One thing Littlewood did do was to bring in to play that element of vaudeville in English acting. Her influence on other directors is fairly minimal. There are a tribe of people who have tried to reproduce the style of theatre which she created, but if you look at the mainstream of theatre, the National or the RSC, it has nothing to do with Joan Littlewood. She was a great director, a phenomenon, but she didn't percolate British theatre. If you drop into any repertory in the country you won't see the hand of Joan Littlewood.

Stage conventions are not uninfluenced by fashion (or fad): Littlewood tore down the proscenium arch; successive directors and actors have carefully and conscientiously rebuilt it. But the design, lighting and make-up techniques which were initiated, or at the very least perfected, at Stratford are now accepted by every theatre and producer. Movement and dance were not the prerogative of the Theatre Royal, but Stratford was the first major venue to incorporate them into stage acting. Jim Hiley, author of *Theatre at Work,* studied Theatre at university before the subject was recognized as a proper academic discipline in Britain. Then, in the mid 1980s, Joan Littlewood's name was on everybody's lips.

All students of theatre, actors, directors and any person in any way connected with theatre was excited about Brecht at the time. What Joan Littlewood demonstrated was that Brecht could work in English terms, she showed that it could succeed, and provided the evidence. On fringe theatre her influence has had a long range, possibly not so much otherwise. She was a teacher, and her example is more significant than the actual productions which took place at Workshop. Arnold Wesker and Centre 42 never managed to keep going, she did.

As well as the accurate and truthful interpretation of the work at Stratford, there has been among some, complete misunderstanding of what went on, resulting in allegedly Workshop-influenced productions which have been disasters. Because the company at the Theatre Royal appeared to be making lines up as they went along, and because of the fluidity of their performances, naïve observers believed the secret to be lack of rehearsal. That was far from the truth. So the ostensible informality of Joan Littlewood's productions has on occasion given rise to simple inefficiency in the guise of improvisation.

It has been said that Stratford was the first theatre to stop pretending that the audience didn't exist. Communication is now an indispensible term in any director's vocabulary, before the Second World War it would have been declamation. Joan Littlewood was not solely responsible for the transformation, but she did a great deal to help.

Kenneth Tynan came close to giving a definitive review of Workshop's achievement back in 1956 when he wrote of Brendan Behan's *The Quare Fellow*. He concluded his piece:

> John Bury's two sets exactly capture the aridity of confinement. And Joan Littlewood's production is the best advertisement for Theatre Workshop that I have yet seen: a model of restraint, integrity, and disciplined naturalism. Glynn Edwards, Brian Murphy, and Maxwell Shaw, as three of Her Majesty's guests, and Dudley Foster, as one of the same lady's uninformed hosts, stand out from an inspired all-male company. Miss Littlewood's cast knows perfectly well what it is doing. She must now devote a few rehearsals to making sure that we can understand precisely what it is saying. That done, *The Quare Fellow* will belong not only in such transient records as this, but in theatrical history.

3.
After Workshop

It is impossible to give a precise date for the ending of Theatre Workshop, and choosing an approximate one has to be an arbitrary decision. The title was retained at Stratford East until 1978. Some will argue that true Workshop style did not survive the 1960s, others will debate long and hard that *Oh. What a Lovely War* was the final gasp. Most of this is of interest only to the pedant. Joan Littlewood and Gerry Raffles were Theatre Workshop, their companies and productions were only expressions of it. When Raffles died and Littlewood left, little or none of Workshop remained.

Ken Hill had established a lasting and widespread reputation with his intensely researched and cleverly balanced shows about female pirates and lands full of dinosaurs. Gerry Raffles had given his blessing to this approach before he left the theatre and box office receipts and encouraging notices seemed to support Ken Hill. But he was never really happy in the position of artistic director – 'I was pitchforked into it, never had any real philosophy other than a vague area I wanted to tread – and was forced to manage, direct and write all at the same time.

Hill brought in an administrator, Caroline Eves, to help him as a junior partner. But with a quantity of pressure which no modern theatre controller would even contemplate, his work began to suffer. Joan Littlewood's behaviour was erratic and sometimes completely unbalanced after Raffles's death, and she turned against Hill during his period in charge. She then threatened to sue Caroline Eves for an alleged, and extremely unlikely, derogatory remark about Gerry Raffles.

With third-hand reports of Littlewood's criticisms reaching the artistic director from sources as unlikely as the theatre cleaner, the situation became intolerable.

I had to resign, clearly. It was also a specific decision made after talking to a lot of people, with the object of bringing Joan to her senses. She was acting very strangely. Looking back on it I may have been better off weathering that period, but at the time I sincerely believed that she needed some cold water thrown over her. It had no effect. We were friends again a year later.

A series of meetings took place in the homes of Philip Hedley, Maxwell Shaw and Shelagh Delaney to bring some sort of order to the theatre. Known as the Steering Committee, this *ad hoc* group consisted of up to thirty actors, writers, directors and academics with an interest in Stratford. Littlewood hoped that out of these discussions a new manager or team of directors would form, and resurrect Theatre Workshop. The outcome of most of the meetings was a request for Littlewood herself to return to the theatre, which was exactly what she did not want. Philip Hedley and Shelagh Delaney, together and individually, were named as possible directors at Stratford but nobody seemed willing to take on such a difficult and potentially unrewarding task.

The Sunday meetings became responsible for putting on a short season at the theatre, with mixed results. *Look Out, It's Sir* by Stephen Lewis, in July 1975, prompted Irving Wardle to write in *The Times*:

> As usual, the show begins well before you get inside. On what used to be the car park Joan Littlewood has set up a 'Kids' Village' consisting of garishly painted odds and ends. The Waltham Forest Jewish Girl Bagpipers were out in force, in competition with a man singing Verdi at the door.
>
> It sounds quite jolly when you write it down. In fact, it feels sadder every time. Marooned among the encroaching tower blocks, the Theatre Royal has got to the stage of treating everything, including the chance of its own destruction, as an invitation to belly laughs. On Monday there was even a mock demolition team assaulting the walls with a plastic boulder. One can well imagine this management organizing a knees-up on the Titanic.

After praising aspects of the production *Financial Times* critic Michael Coveney spoke for many when he said: 'I am fast losing patience with this house's perennial insistence that an alternative life to drab reality is to be had in penthouses or even careers with Woolworth's'

A proposed Shelagh Delaney play failed to materialize, and it took a one-man show from Ron Moody, *Move Along Sideways*, to save the box office. Ken Campbell and his Road Show played at the beginning of October (star member Sylveste McCoy had been an early discovery at Stratford) but short idiosyncratic shows were not sufficient to maintain a full-scale theatre. Maxwell Shaw remembers a telephone call from a depressed Joan Littlewood.

> She reiterated that she would never come back, and at the same time felt
> awful about the theatre being in such a poor way. Now, Joan can be so sweet
> when she really wants something – she told me that she would feel secure if I
> took over just for a few months, that I was the only one and so on. So I
> agreed, but only for the short term, to manage the theatre.

Shaw had directed in rep and had been responsible for *Sweeney Todd* and *The
Italian Straw Hat* at Stratford, and although the former had been a notable
success, Littlewood saw him as an administrator rather than a director.
London-born, art-school educated and forty-six years old when he took over,
Shaw's task at the Theatre Royal was to be even more arduous than he had
imagined.

When the appointment was announced Joan Littlewood helped to draft a
statement and a press conference was held. There was much talk of a 'new era'
and the 'spirit of Raffles and Littlewood'. Shaw stated that his policy was to
initiate a season of 'optimistic plays, with direct relevance to today'. Stress was
to be put on uncluttered direction rather than intricate touches, the guiding
tones were simplicity and honesty. The season opened in November with Mrs
Gaskell's *Cranford,* adapted by Littlewood and John Wells. Milton Shulman,
rarely the darling of the acting profession but on this occasion quite just,
eschewed the euphemisms of his fellow critics when he surveyed the production
in the *Evening Standard*:

> There may have been a time when a musical based upon the leisurely and
> gentle activities of the ladies of Cranford, as recorded in Mrs Gaskell's
> well-known novel, would have had an appreciative and amused audience.
>
> But in these abrasive, jangling and violent days, I doubt if there will be
> much understanding or interest in these prim little ladies in Cheshire in the
> 1850s, gossiping and tea-drinking and day-dreaming their uneventful and
> relatively innocent lives away.
>
> The unlikely adaptors of this bucolic idyll are Joan Littlewood and John
> Wells, who have admirably retained most of the novel's salient events as well
> as its predominant mood of feminine gentility.
>
> But at the Theatre Royal, Stratford, last night, all the fluttering and
> regretting and middle-class restraint seemed too sugary for consumption and
> too soporific for sustained attention.
>
> Miss Matilda Jenkyns flash-backs through her old letters to the days when
> she was dissuaded from marrying the rich farmer Holbrook because he was

not considered a gentleman by her family.

After that traumatic decision, Matty's life in Cranford was made up of such exciting incidents as a cow falling into a lime pit, a smoking chimney during a tea party, a visit from a travelling conjuror, the arrival of some imaginary robbers, the marriage of a grand lady to an uncouth local doctor, the loss of her money, and the final arrival of her long lost brother to save her from penury.

Joan Kemp-Welch's direction telescopes these bitty occasions into a series of charming encounters that are not too cluttered up by the songs of Carl Davis, with mildly inventive lyrics by John Wells.

But the tune are so determinately period in feeling that they hit a consistently monotonous trilly and tinkly note.

Penelope Lee as Miss Matty smiles courageously through her development from mousy young girl to mousy old spinster. Pamela Charles and Stephanie Voss chatter vigorously away as the town gossips and snobs.

For all the ardent work put into this small musical, *Cranford,* I'm afraid, is a misconceived idea that will bore far more people than it amuses. It may have a future as an annual students play in a girls' school where its gentility and its dependance on a predominant female cast could prove an attraction.

The unfortunate choice for the opening show of the season set a style both in character and quality which was to make the rest of Maxwell Shaw's time in control of the theatre an uphill struggle. The Christmas production, *Nickleby and Me* with book and lyrics by Caryl Brahms and Ned Sherrin, had more supporters but still failed to make any significant impact. Concerts took place on weekends in an effort to ease the financial situation and rebuild local participation, and a critics' forum in January 1976 had a distinctly Workshop feel about it with its attempt to break away from the traditional image of the remote and untouchable theatre commentator.

In February came a production which destroyed any hope the new administration may have had of securing either financial or critical success. Christopher Bond's *Judge Jeffreys* received massive publicity before its run thanks to actor Simon Williams having recently achieved international fame as Major Bellamy in the television series 'Upstairs, Downstairs'. The production was seen to be, and those at the theatre did nothing to destroy the illusion, as a test case – money, time and talent had been put into an important play at an important venue. The result was a disaster. Nicholas de Jongh said of it in the *Guardian*:

This, in its closing stages, is a filthy little play and its earlier scenes are

This Jockey Drives Late Tonight, 1980. The height of mediocrity

Davis and Keeffe outside the theatre. Most critics wish that they had stayed there

Alf Garnett and his thoughts

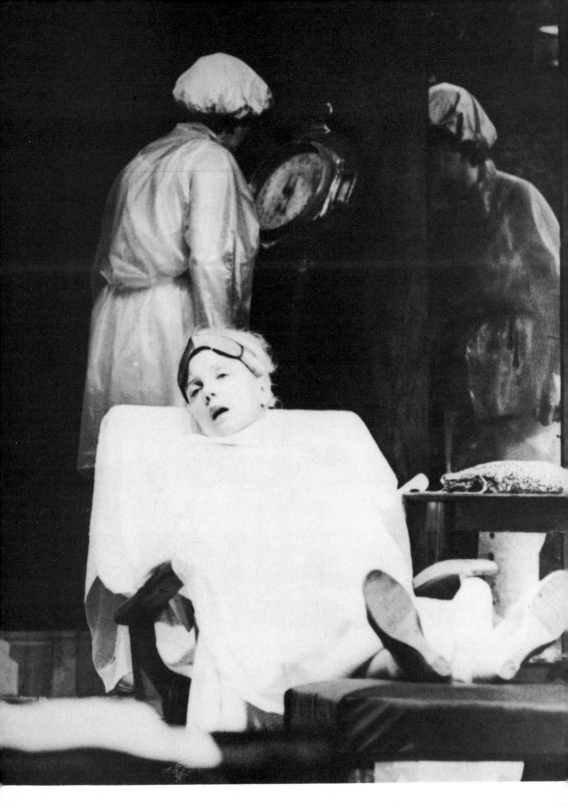

Steaming, 1980

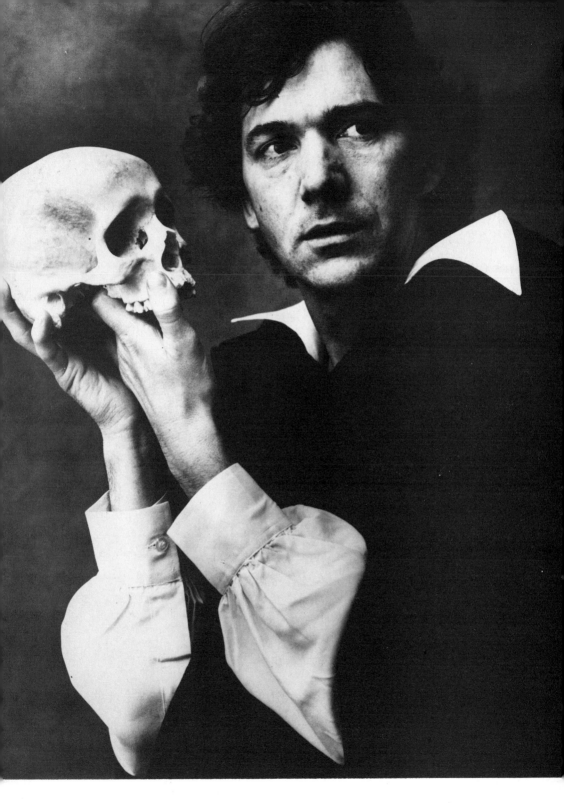

Frank Grimes: 'Hamlet on a rubbish tip'

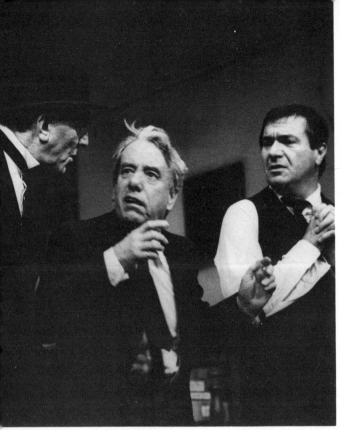

Almost a transfer: *Stiff Options,* 1982

32

Writer and stars of *On Your Way Riley* in director Hedley's flat

33

marked by a kind of ill-informed, dramatically inept silliness which suggests that the author, Christopher Bond, knows nothing of the religious intensities and divisions, the political and constitutional crises which marked and marred the transition from Charles II to James II, the 1688 'Revolution'. Mr Bond has, however, said that he wants people to come away from the theatre 'feeling good about life. I want a man to come away feeling like he wanted to go to bed with his wife'. On this evidence he is aiming too high: he will be lucky if he fired anyone with any sort of sexual passion. And good feelings? Conceit has its limits.

There is a final section in *Judge Jeffreys* which emerges loosely from what has gone before: Ron Yates, played by that very upstairs actor Simon Williams as if imitating one of Peter Cook's funny country voices, and Wozzie, an endearing young country person, wait for execution, both victims of James II's Anglican persecutions. The expression of that is conveyed in a preliminary description of cauldron, ropes, and maiming, fulfilled in a hanging scene where the men are topped. This is presented in gruesome detail, and interspersed with Bond's characteristic cheap anachronism: a death speech is received with 'Very good, you ought to go on New Faces'. The executioner sings, 'I did it my way'.

Unless for some moral or satirical advantage I do not see that the physical and graphic presentation of a hanging has any justification: here it looks nothing but obscenely irrelevant in its lingering detail and aimless in purpose. For the rest *Judge Jeffreys* is a fragile, occasional chronicle of a west country, into which the demented hanging judge, played by Howard Southern, intrudes. The language and situation are cheaply 1970s, though with such occasional and aimless intent this does not matter, the Duke of York and Monmouth travestied is appropriate for something which is ignorance throughout, a kind of reduced Carry On Country Folk. Michael Halsey's Wozzie is most endearing. The director is Maxwell Shaw and his choice of plays can only improve.

It did. But not enough to change opinion formulated in the first few months. *An Italian Straw Hat* was revived, largely out of desperation, and Georges Feydeau's *Out of Practice,* again directed by Shaw, and again attacked by the critics, was treated with indifference by the public. A production of Kurosawa's *Rashomon* fared little better. By the autumn of 1976 Shaw was anxious to leave the theatre.

Even eight years after the event he does not know exactly why things went so badly. 'It was difficult to find the right actors, and notes and letters from Joan without her actually being there were no real help. I did the best I could, what else can I say? When business became very poor I had to bring in guest productions, that was the time to leave'. Maxwell Shaw cannot take all the blame: the job of artistic director had been available; nobody had the courage or the faith to take it on. Shaw, under protest, did.

As a concerned, intellectual man his reputation for gentleness and integrity is unimpeachable; it is doubtful however if these were the attributes needed to drag a once great theatre out of decay. When John Bury, never a harsh critic, suggested in the minutes of a theatre meeting that Maxwell Shaw had not done well at Stratford, Shaw was deeply hurt. Bury was accurate, though, and it was up to those who had any belief in the future of Stratford East to select a young, able director who could expunge the aura of gloom and put the theatre on a firm artistic and financial footing.

Clare Venables had had experience as an actress and director both at the Lincoln theatre and as a freelance when she came to Stratford East to direct a Christmas production of Ken Campbell's *Old King Cole*. Maxwell Shaw offered her the production, with the proviso that it should be ready in two weeks and the budget should not exceed a certain derisory sum. She accepted, satisfied both requirements and made a lasting impression on Maxwell Shaw. It had been Philip Hedley, who had worked with Venables at Lincoln, who had recommended her for the job, and he was on the board of the Theatre Royal when Maxwell Shaw announced that he strongly recommended that Clare Venables take over the artistic directorship of Stratford East. Her appointment went through, informally and quickly.

The difficulties she faced had to do with more than policy and approach. As the first person to administer the theatre who had not been involved with Theatre Workshop, and being a woman, the media wasted little time in comparing her with Joan Littlewood, and to her detriment. She had been warned. Although Littlewood was still very much alive, it was as if her ghost stalked the dressing-rooms and corridors of Stratford. Venables was seen by many as an outsider, and was resented for it. The accusation of 'Joan would never have done it that way' was to haunt her throughout her years in the job.

'If all of the people who claimed to have worked with Joan Littlewood really had done, Theatre Workshop would have had a cast of thousands', she points out. 'There were people there who were not prepared to let me succeed. It was almost as if I had to fail, to prove a point.' The board of governors at the theatre at the time showed little objection to any of Clare Venables's measures, but offered little help either.

Her plan was to escape from the confines of constantly looking back to the victories of the past. Local audiences and local issues were to play a central part in the seasons at Stratford. She commissioned writers from outside London to come to the East End to research a particular subject, and then compose a related play. David Holman and Rony Robinson were two of the writers she commissioned, and Holman's *Dig for Victory* was one result of the project. The reviews, in the summer of 1978, were favourable. Ned Chaillet wrote in *The Times*:

> Half the audiences for London theatres are said to be tourists, filling up the better seats in the West End and keeping plays going for the rest of us. They are not likely to be travelling out on the Central Line to the Theatre Royal, Stratford East, to see a play about Britain during the Second World War. Chances are they would not understand everything that was being said, although it is the British politics of the time that might prove more impenetrable than the cockney accents of David Holman's characters.
>
> Even so, Mr Holman, who must have been born at about the end of the war, has things of some importance to say about Britain. The hopes of his cockney Labour supporter for a socialist Britain do not need to be dashed in the play, since the slightest knowledge of present reality will do that for him, and his explicit portraiture of the East End survival after the Blitz is full of similarity ironical snapshots which depend on our view from the present.
>
> The victory garden that his characters build out of the rubble of a bomb site is demolished by black marketeers when victory brings tightened rations instead of plenty and there is not always joy felt for the returning soldiers by the women who have learnt to live without them. But his play is not finally without hope and throughout it is rich in humanity and good humour, with as much sympathy for John Halstead's profiteering spiv as for the Yankee soldier who courts Margot Leicester's war widow and the Jewish child refugee who never speaks above a whisper.
>
> Mr Holman's play, by focussing on that time when Britain was united and victorious, tells us much about the present. He may not look so deeply into individuals as Stephen Lowe did in his recent wartime drama, *Touched*, but his panoramic sweep, in Sebastian Born's production, is far from superficial.

Sandy Craig ended his *Time Out* review with the significant 'Nevertheless, this marks a true return to form for the Theatre Workshop who serve the play well with some beautifully pitched and controlled performances.'

For the first time the new artistic director was in the spotlight at a national level, with most of her productions receiving blanket coverage and reviews in every quality newspaper and magazine. And although Clare Venables had a genuine concern for East London and its inhabitants, contact between the theatre and the local people was more difficult, less natural, than it had seemed in previous years.

An early triumph, and a production which was representative of Venables and the people she employed at their best, was the seasonal pantomime in 1977. Directed by Martin Duncan, also responsible for *Milady's Silver Musick* to celebrate the royal jubilee, *The Amusing Spectacle of Cinderella and Her Naughty-Naughty Sisters* broke box-office records. John Barber wrote in the *Daily Telegraph*:

> If anyone thinks London pantomime is dead, let them hasten to the Theatre Royal, Stratford E, where a delightful new 'Cinderella' has a packed house of children roaring approval and, what is unusual, held spellbound by the story.
>
> I do mean new. Martin Duncan's book and lyrics are fresh as paint. No blue joke, no routine slap-stick, no single charts-topper and no television gag interrupts the flow of original ideas. The best are excellent.
>
> The band, for example, is a family of Chico-ish Italians who cook spaghetti in the intervals and dispute fiercely about the plot. At one point they have to stuff the piano with new notes because the music has run out.
>
> The grotesque costumes of David Fisher also contribute to a visual effect that recalls Tenniel, especially as worn by two splendid clowns — Needle and Fred (Vincent Brimble and Robert Pugh), of whom we might see more.
>
> Then there are two elegant blackamoor compères. The plot has new twists: the cruel step-mother orders our heroine to teach cockroaches to dance — and she does so in style. And the language has a fruity charm ('I'm naught but an honest old beldame').
>
> Admittedly, Mr Martin's wit is more willing than able. He will labour such names as Prince Fritz Fitz-Pince and his steward Dandy-Knee (who has a pretty joint). On the other hand — 'Since I met you I have thought of little else,' says the Prince. 'Don't call me Little Else,' Cinderella demurs. We could have done with more in this regrettable vein.
>
> Pauline Siddle simpers as Cinders, and Susan Jameson is her rather colourless Prince. But Darlene Johnson makes a rich, ripe good fairy, and Felicity Harrison's Dandy-Knee is as pretty a swaggerer as you could want.
>
> Above all, children were riveted, and could understand every word. It is, of course, a rough, tough East End theatre where everyone knows everyone else.

Venables disappointed board members and theatre workers by failing to exploit those successes. She neither backed them by effective publicity nor used them to build an imaginative public relations campaign. It is significant that on the shelves of the current press and publicity office of the Theatre Royal the only time not covered by scrapbooks reviews and articles is the first two years of Clare Venables's stint as artistic director. This was partly due to lack of finance, but also because of a shift in values. The red carnation worn on first nights by theatre staff and the attention paid to detail by Gerry Raffles had established the 'audience as guests, not customers' approach which was to continue only after Venables had left. She broke the traditions, and traditions play an integral part in the life of Stratford East.

I may have taken too hard a line at the time [she said later], that might be true. I was in love with the area and with the building but I disliked it living off the past, the future seemed to be much more important. My policy changed. At first it was to put on local plays and stage socialist classics, that went by the board. In my second year there I had a baby, my hormones were zooming around all over the place. Some of what went wrong was my fault: I can be impatient. One production failed to take place, I had a couple of bad flops. But the *Guardian* said after one play that I'd pulled, at one stroke, the theatre out of the post-Littlewood haze. I'd defend that. I was the first me, not the second Joan Littlewood, yet if a production came off I'd be told 'that was reminiscent of Workshop', and if it failed they'd say 'Well, it wasn't Theatre Workshop, was it'.

Part of her radical approach towards the problems at Stratford East was to bring in three new permanent officials at the theatre. Jonathan Chadwick became associate director, Jules Wright assistant director and Rony Robinson writer-in-residence. One of the theories behind the move was for Venables and her two directors to rotate power between themselves – an idea which was never seriously implemented and could never have succeeded in dealings with bodies such as the Arts Council. By the beginning of 1979 dissent was being voiced, but loyalty to Venables and her staff was still quite strong from those who worked with her on a day-to-day basis. Audience figures were not encouraging and the Theatre Board, few of whom were regular visitors, expressed its concern.

Joan Littlewood was being fed reports of tension and unhappiness throughout this period. The incident which sparked off a protracted argument and the eventual resignation of Clare Venables was innocuous and absurd. While visiting a hospital, Littlewood was approached by a porter who congratulated her on the theatre of old and wondered why it had gone downhill so rapidly. For all she knew the man could have been repeating unfounded gossip, but she decided to launch what Maxwell Shaw describes as a 'Get rid of Clare Venables thing, with all the people that she'd taken on on mid- and long-term contracts'.

Littlewood, who was at the time receiving an annual rent of £6,000 from the theatre, had not seen a production at Stratford for years, and had no real knowledge of Clare Venables and her methods. This did not seem to matter, and after a round of frantic telephone calls the Theatre Board and an ex-director had brought the administration to the verge of collapse.

In September 1979 Venables was occupied with coming productions and the raising of £200,000 for essential structural repairs to the building. She was aware of some disquiet – it would have been impossible to have been ignorant of it – but mass criticism and censure were not in the air. Littlewood called a meeting of those members of the board whom she saw as firm allies, in a Chenies Street office and the 'poor' work of Clare Venables was discussed in detail. Philip Hedley decided to call an emergency meeting of the full board.

Venables was telephoned and told what was happening, and was also informed that until the accusations of inefficiency were made to a full and properly constructed board meeting they were unofficial. Matters were not made any easier by the fact that it was Hedley who had made these calls. He had already been in dispute with Clare Venables when they were both at Lincoln and although he had spoken for her in the past, a barrier of distrust remained. Today she refuses to comment on Philip Hedley or on his actions during the dispute, and he – describing himself as 'a mixture of naïveté and Machiavellianism' – will say only that although his involvement was purely as a mediator, the overall treatment of Clare Venables was unfair.

The board meeting took place at County Hall, with Venables looking both shaken and upset, and hiding behind dark glasses. It was the first time she had come face to face with Joan Littlewood. Littlewood amazed all present by making a gushing speech expressing sympathy for Clare Venables, explaining how she understood the pressures of running Stratford and how thankless the task could be. Venables produced a typewritten statement, said her piece and left the room.

The statement read as follows:

This meeting is the end of an intolerable process. There is a board meeting and AGM in 10 days time and yet I have been called to a meeting to discuss the future policy and direction of the theatre, something we spend a large part of our working day at the theatre on, and should be part of our regular board meetings, and I am phoned by the Chairman with a series of failings to be answered in some way. The manner in which this situation has been handled, whatever this situation is about, indicates the breakdown of the functioning of this board.

I have spent 2½ years at the Theatre Royal. The manner of my appointment was casual, though charming. Attendance at, and handling of board meetings has always been casual. What the casualness has masked is that the board has not done its job, though individuals may be well meaning. In many ways, and I have indicated this as politely as possible at various board meetings, I have been left to get on with it. There have never been any decent discussions of the present day or future policy; there has never been any criticism. OK if that's how you wanted it to be, but if you don't get involved at all in the policy or let me know your criticisms of it, I have to assume I think that you are basically in tune with what I'm doing, even though I might be heavily critical of my own work at various times. Having suddenly decided that you want to ACT in some way, you throw our work into disarray by calling this meeting in the way you did, summon me to it with a list of ignorant accusations and expect me to sit here calmly and discuss your problems. I have been working *on your behalf* I stress, for 2½ years, and I have had successes in many quarters and have taken my work seriously. One of the things the Chairman wants to discuss is the rebuilding and fund-raising . . . are you capable of it as a board?

I take this as an example of my problems. Acting on instructions from an earlier meeting, I have *already* been interviewing fund raisers, and set the architect and surveyors to work. We are preparing our long and detailed applications to all our funding bodies. The Arts Council meets on 24 September, the local authorities have promised help and want meetings to discuss the details etc. and how we will handle it. It's not a *game*. I've been working on it *seriously*. I have been your representative in dealing with public bodies and firms. But I cannot trust *you* any longer as a public body and therefore the work has no foundation. I do not trust you as a board to go through the difficult time ahead in the best way for the theatre.

Your inadequacies as a board as far as I am concerned culminate in the events leading up to and the calling of this meeting, and make it quite impossible for me to continue my duties another minute in the present situation. The policy in train at the theatre, constantly developing, having its bad time and its good, is, I believe, the right one, difficult, dangerous but solid. I hope for your, and the theatre's, and my colleagues' sake you continue with it, but I can no longer continue as the situation stands.

Strident as the document was, it did not state categorically that Venables was resigning. Philip Hedley, the only person to come out of the unpleasant sequence of events with anything approaching innocence, was sent to find out. 'If we'd taken a vote before Clare had given the statement, at the beginning of the meeting the majority would probably have been for her', he explained. 'As it was the best she could have got was half a dozen votes, not enough to keep her job.' Hedley contacted her, and indeed she had resigned. Hedley then resigned as board chairman and accepted the artistic directorship on a temporary basis.

The position of Jules Wright and Jonathan Chadwick was precarious, not to say unworkable. Hedley wrote to Chadwick, with his analysis of the situation:

For all I've spent more time with you than anybody else on the staff, I still haven't completed all the talk necessary I'm sure.

But now I have some measure of what needs doing, I've absolutely got to get on with it fast. The box-office figures for 'Puntila' and the enclosed letter from the GLC have added to the urgency of the situation, and I must have a full staff ready and willing to cope with the urgent situation from Monday onwards.

I've given you some idea of my stop-gap programme. Immediate commercial decision will only become more drastic in the light of the GLC letter. The original job outlined for you this autumn doing the artistic planning is, as you have said, no longer relevant. The associate director's job, in current circumstances, and taking into account the job responsibilities over the past year, would be mainly administrative, coping with the Arts Council figures, rebuilding, booking artists etc. and being thrown into any breach that appears. I must know by the end of today if you can do this job as I have to decide whether or not to employ a stop-gap administrator.

Chadwick's response was unequivocal, and provoked a second letter from Hedley:

In view of your action in my office yesterday in front of the technical staff when you tore up my letter regarding current work that needs to be done, plus the copy of the GLC letter appertaining to next year's grant, I have no alternative but to suspend you as from today's date until the board has discussed your letter of resignation and decided on your future with us.

Both Chadwick and Wright resigned, leaving Philip Hedley with a three-month period to fill. The agreement was that he would cancel a show intended for the Arts Theatre and take over control of Stratford until a full-time

A Star is Torn. Robyn Archer: magnificent

Prayers weren't fully answered in *Any Minute Now*   35

Welcome Home Jacko, 1983

A box office catastrophe for *Gas and Candles,* 1983

director could be found. Finding first-class productions to put on at a moment's notice was no easy task – today it would be even more difficult – and Hedley went to writers and performers whom he knew had some connection with, or penchant for, Stratford East.

Mustapha Matura's play about young Rastafarians, *Welcome Home Jacko*, was brought in, as was *Sus* by Barrie Keeffe – who was born locally, and was to write the screenplay for *The Long Good Friday* and other plays at Stratford. Hedley also brought in Warren Mitchell and Johnny Speight's *The Thoughts of Chairman Alf*. It was a powerful combination for such a short preparation time, reviews were good and morale rose. The Alf Garnett show did particularly well, and transferred to the West End. Warren Mitchell has clear memories of it:

> The idea had been around for quite some time to do a show on the lines of a monologue of Alf and his views. Speight phoned me up, mentioned that Stratford would be a good place, and then told me he was going on a golfing holiday – would I have a go at getting some things together? The first run through of the show was four and a half hours long, to cut out two hours was very hard indeed. Reviews were great, I didn't use a microphone and the rapport with the audience was perfect. I remember in the middle of one male chauvinistic bit I was doing, a large lady who looked like a post-card caricature stood up and shouted 'Men! I've had three husbands, pissed 'em all off. Who needs 'em.' Then the audience joined in. I wanted to ask her to come back the second night.

Hedley followed up the three successes with a variety bill featuring Annie Ross and George Melly, and a Ken Hill pantomime starring Brian Murphy. The theatre was still experiencing difficulties following the departure of a complete managerial staff and several actors, and Hedley continued to see his reign as purely temporary. He then underwent a conversion on the road to Leytonstone.

> From feeling depressed as I walked up the front ramp into the theatre, two incidents occurred which changed my way of thinking: I rushed out of my flat one morning, worried about being late for work – I realized that I was actually looking forward to it. And then as I pinned up the posters from my first few shows I felt proud, like a shopkeeper displaying his wares. I wanted to stay.

Born in Manchester in 1938, Hedley had been educated in London and Australia. After theatrical experience in Liverpool, Watford, Birmingham and

Lincoln, he worked as a freelance director from 1974, moving to areas as diverse as Canada and the Sudan. At Stratford he was seen as a liberal-minded, pleasant young man who used to be Joan and Gerry's assistant, and hence no threat. But his initial approach was to be a spirited and aggressive one: within the first month he was walking around Stratford precinct with a large sandwich board advertising the theatre, much to the chagrin of the resident publicity officer.

Two early productions which strengthened his hand at Stratford were *A Short Sharp Shock* and *The Streets of London*, both taking place in the first season of 1980 and the latter transferring, with much less success, to Her Majesty's in the Haymarket. In a letter to Joan Littlewood, Hedley wrote:

> The good news is that the anti-Thatcher show, *A Short Sharp Shock*, had a tremendous box office success. Two neanderthal Tory MPs objected to it and demanded we had our grant cut. One of them went on TV and held up a poster for the show, explained it started the next night at Stratford East and told people firmly that they should not attend it. The result, packed houses. Questions were asked in the House, the Arts Council issued statements, threatening letters were received by the cast. It was all great fun.

Doubtless unrelated, but still a great shock, was a meeting at the Arts Council which Hedley was asked to attend. An understanding committee asked if the problems and past disasters at Stratford made the future hopeless and any further work and financing a waste of time. The question was partly rhetorical. The artistic director of only a few months' standing left the meeting a worried man.

In September *The Curse of the Mummy's Tomb* received grudgingly mediocre reviews, with Hugo Davenport in the *Guardian* being the most encouraging.

> The Mummy's Tomb, described as a musical horror show, was unwrapped at the Theatre Royal, Stratford East on Thursday. It is one of London's less sepulchral theatrical offerings – an enjoyable blend of B-movie and Vaudeville which, if it does not exactly break new ground, succeeds admirably in creating a kind of Pharaohic farce.
>
> In a sense, its success is guaranteed, given a certain level of adroitness on the part of the performers. The cinematic mythology of mummies is universal, allowing writer–director Ken Hill to tell a story which gives off the pleasing glow of total familiarity. The techniques of vaudeville have an equally broad appeal. And there can be no doubt that the performers inject enough life into it to revive even the most torpid of Egyptian effigies.
>
> All the traditional ingredients are here. The play carries us from Professor

Niven's study to a warehouse in Wapping, across the ocean and up the Nile in a dhow, to the vast tunnels of the mummy's tomb. There are cobras, camels, treacherous Egyptians, and deranged Englishmen – all interspersed with delightfully fresh and witty song and dance routines.

Adrienne Posta, as the professor's indomitable daughter on her fourteenth fiancé, tinkles away to great effect in the impeccable accent of Roedean. To Miss Posta, too, goes the credit for some pretty crisp choreography. Anna Sharkey, who plays both an Irish housekeeper and a 3,500 year old priestess, is all snakelike sibilance. Her singing is superb: she has a really fine voice which lends itself well to operatic pastiche. The band is first-class, effortlessly switching from one style to another.

There is, however, some tightening up to be done in the second act – in particular, during the climactic scene when three mummies (one real, two fake) are chasing each other through the Necropolis.

The theatre has been decorated throughout with amusing imitations of Egyptian tomb paintings, and the programme boasts a remarkably eclectic list of acknowledgements. The list of credits includes the Post Office, the Salvation Army, Moet and Chandon, the Egyptian Embassy, and the Clay Pigeon Association, among others.

The following month Philip Hedley directed his first play for two years at Stratford. Not in the mainstream of career conscious and ambitious directors, his devotion to overall theatre policy rather than personal directorial success has been one of his most attractive attributes. Unfortunately *This Jockey Drives Late Nights,* Henry Livings's updated version of Tolstoy's *The Power of Darkness,* reflected his lack of directorial ambition. Reviews were damning and, although the production improved, the box office suffered quite badly.

The Christmas pantomime for 1980 was *Robin Hood* with Toni Palmer, Sylveste McCoy and Bill Wallis. The *Guardian* described it as 'A hoot. A palpable hoot', and children agreed. Earlier in December an ambitious plan to enlarge the scope of Stratford finally materialized. Following the line of the Royal Court's Upstairs, the Hammersmith Lyric's Studio and Stratford upon Avon's The Other Place, Hedley gave the go-ahead for a small studio theatre at the back of the main auditorium to be used as a second venue. Youngsters in the area named it The Square Thing, and young writer Tony Marchant opened the season with his *Remember Me.*

Jim Hiley, writing in *Time Out,* was most impressed.

The twin debuts of playwright Tony Marchant and Stratford East's new studio make for one of the happiest fringe events in a long time. The young unemployed anti-heroes of Marchant's piece – neither of them very proficient villains – break into the school one of them attended and steal fifteen quid. They then debate whether to stay and wreak revenge on the place – Mick's vague but angry intention – or get out while the going's good, as counselled by the less earnest Saff. Underlying this edgy altercation is the general question of what they will do with their seemingly prospectless lives, and the implicit answer is neither dispiriting nor simply reassuring. With frequent flash-backs to the recent past, the play's construction is a little self-conscious; but the writing is witty, true and powerfully rhythmic. Director Adrian Shergold has elicited astonishingly convincing performances from John Fowler and Andrew Paul, and this intricate, thoughtful dialogue is a welcome addition to the repertoire of a company that tends to specialize in the broad and loud.

The Greater London Council was not as enthusiastic, and after discovering that the venue was not, as had been thought, a theatre club and was a fire-trap to boot, it was closed after just eighteen months. The Square Thing now exists only as a spare rehearsal room – a poor reward for having given life to the first plays of promising young writers.

While Hedley was concentrating on financial reform and on arranging a new season, he received the news that the Arts Council, in its eternal wisdom, had decided to put the Theatre Royal on a danger list; Stratford East had one year to prove itself deserving of public support and backing. Unfortunately, the featured production of the period was Barrie Keeffe and Ray Davis's *Chorus Girls,* which managed to annoy every critic in the auditorium. A normally sympathetic Steve Grant did not hide his distaste when writing in *Time Out*:

Barrie Keeffe and Ray Davis have reworked Aristophanes with an eye for rock music, police corruption, East End geography, royal weddings and the SAS and come up with *Chorus Girls.* It's a crushingly disappointing affair, scrappy, puerile, badly directed, drowned by its good intentions, flattened by its pulled punches and caught squarely between two stalls. Does it lean towards good fun or serious point-making; trendy topicality or salty music-hall traditionalism? Is Marc Sinden's Prince Charles, kidnapped willingly by a bunch of Theatre Royal chorus ladies, a chinless twit or sinister aristocratic stud; is Charlotte Cornwell's spokesdame a feminist heroine, a figure of fun or (as I suspect) just an awful misconception which had my moderate female companion chewing her ticket stub with fury? And if there's talk of unemployment, wife-beating, sieges, graft and the like, why settle for such a wretched, simplistic SingalongaDavies ending? And after thirty minute who cares? Sadly only in the occasional Davies song, the intermittent telling line from Keeffe and a few good performances (particularly Michael Elphick's bumptious copper and Lesley Manville in the titular line) are there compensations. This is just not good enough — especially not when the people for whom it was written can now stay at home and watch sophisticated, well-produced, popular programmes on the box.

Kate Williams, born in East Ham and trained at the E15 Acting School, was in the show. She played an alcoholic nymphomaniac.

I was supposed to be the Lady Mayoress of Newham, spending most of the night trying to get into Prince Charles's knickers. What is difficult to understand is that a lot of talent had been pulled together for it, when we first looked at it we thought it would be a big hit, and everybody worked bloody hard to get it right. We just didn't, and I'm still not entirely sure why.

Philip Hedley was now in a position to implement some of his earlier promises to both the Arts Council and the theatregoing public. He had spoken of prestigious actors and directors coming to Stratford, and in May of 1981 Lindsay Anderson came to direct *Hamlet*. The man chosen to play the role was Frank Grimes. Irish-born and now resident in the United States, Grimes's career had been largely guided by Anderson. Whatever levels of quality the production may have reached, having a director of Lindsay Anderson's international repute was a *coup* for Hedley and for Stratford. Frank Grimes described his time at the theatre as 'Hamlet on a rubbish tip', but his director is a little more conciliatory:

To say that Stratford is today a continuation of Theatre Workshop or that it is in any way different from any other sympathetic theatre would simply not be true. There's no mystique. Ours was perhaps too ambitious a production for the theatre at that time; a modern classical approach with a sort of Royal Court emphasis on text and a definite anti-Royal Shakespeare feeling.

Physical conditions were difficult, and actor Del Henney, who was criticized for his pedestrian rendering of Claudius, came into the company only four weeks before the opening. Reviews were mixed, and the entire company noticed that few present on the first night had understood the minimalist work of Jocelyn Herbert, a designer of reputation: the less astute among them interpreted the three central pillars on stage as being an indication of the poverty of Stratford East. Michael Billington in the *Guardian* saw some positive aspects in the production; he was not of the majority:

Lindsay Anderson's production of *Hamlet* at the Theatre Royal, Stratford East is the first at this address since 1899; and a perfectly creditable affair it is. Played against a simple Jocelyn Herbert set of three sky-reaching square columns (a homage, I suspect, both to Gordon Craig and a modest budget), it would give anyone seeing the play for the first time a sense of its architecture and its poetry. My own taste is for Shakespeare with a strong directorial concept; but this clear, direct production suggests there is no reason why Stratford-atte-Bowe should not occasionally wrest the Bard from Stratford upon Avon I think.

The best thing about the evening is Frank Grimes's Hamlet. He is not your punk Prince of Denmark Street nor your Lord Alfred Douglas in tights. This Hamlet, Renaissance-garbed and Barrymore-profiled, is dashing and athletic but simply too high-souled to be a revenger. Grimes lets you know he means business by the way he grinds his sword along the floor in 'sweep to my revenge', in his vigorously imagined stabbing of Claudius on 'bloody, bawdy villain' and in his brisk impatience to get the grave scene under way.

But this Hamlet is also a schooled logician who probably got a first in Greats at Wittenberg. He actually wags his finger when telling us that 'conscience does make cowards of us all' as if wrapping up a QED and, when poised over the praying Claudius, there is a fractional pause on 'And so he goes to heaven' as if to suggest another juicy moral problem is on the way. The balance between action and reflection is the hardest thing to hit in Hamlet.

What Grimes admirably gives us is a Prince who is manly, humorous (even standing on his head in front of Polonius) but in the end incapacitated by the over-analytic impulse of the liberal mind.

The rest of the cast is very variable. Cora Kinnaird's Ophelia, as is the modern way, gets bashed about a lot (do drama schools have special combat sessions for budding Ophelias?) and goes mad very unsentimentally: my only doubt is that she signals mental breakdown too early and never suggests a residual passion for the Prince. Del Henney's Claudius is neither bloat nor foxy and actually makes 'It is the poisoned cup' sound as if he is announcing the winner of the 3.30.

But Trevor Martin does a good double as Ghost and first player (he suddenly made me realize how Pyrrhus 'stood, and like neutral to his will and matter, did nothing' is a prefiguration of the Prince) and Peter Holme's Horatio is the kind of fidus Achates to have around in a spiritual crisis.

You don't get much sense of Elsinore, the eavesdroppers' paradise and focus of intrigue from this production nor any implied domestic relationships: Claudius and Gertrude, for instance, have so little physical contact that you don't even feel that for them the postman has rung once. What you do get is a plain narrative account of the play, a good use of minimal resources (the players are obviously having grant trouble with the Danish Arts Council) and a very impressive Hamlet from Mr Grimes.

The best tribute is that the children near to me sat totally attentive to the whole 3½ hours.

Firmly in control of the theatre by the summer of 1981 (some members of staff had been dismissed as part of the process of transforming Stratford from an inefficient harbour of nostalgia into a progressive and forward looking theatre), Hedley issued a policy statement to the Arts Council. A great deal rested on the document's reception.

After 12 months ultimately rewarding struggle to get our house in order administratively and financially a cohesive artistic policy has emerged for Stratford East and this is now coming through in our programme and activities in 1981/82 and is a clear indication of how we will be proceeding in 1982/83.

Our aim is to provide as many and as varied theatrical experiences as possible for the general public and schools in our local borough (Newham) and the boroughs of the north and east with which we are connected by excellent transport facilities. Our current and therefore proposed services for 1982/83 include the following wide range:

A.   THE MAIN STAGE
1.   Home productions of three main types with the very best international talents available
(a)   popular family entertainment such as our annual pantomime, or the Peggy Mount musical proposed for Autumn 1981 or last year's melodrama *The Streets of London*
(b)   more committed and sometimes controversial modern work for which there is an East End audience like the Barrie Keeffe — Ray Davies musical *Chorus Girls* or Nell Dunn's *Steaming* both in the 1981 programme
(c)   the occasional classic like Lindsay Anderson's current production of *Hamlet*.

2.   Visiting fringe companies
Over the past twelve months we've housed numerous leading fringe dramas

and dance companies for one- or two-night stands or in some cases for a week, e.g. 7:84 Scotland. We are becoming a regular annual date for certain dance companies and we are on the GLAA circuit.

3. 'Popular' Sunday nights

Apart from production weekends we are open most Sunday nights and apart from dance and drama events, we present popular entertainers such as Warren Mitchell, George Melly or Bob Kerr's Whoopee Band.

More significantly we present our special Royal Cabarets once a month, a highly original vaudeville/revue/variety evening which is becoming an artistic melting pot for popular entertainment, and a London showcase for artists trying something new. We mean to continue this as a monthly institution and also make it into an annual home production for at least a week's run, aimed particularly at factory outings. Two cabarets a year are staged for Equity causes and our own Building Fund.

B. STUDIO THEATRE

When financially possible we mount small productions in our portakabin studio theatre alongside the main theatre. These inevitably are small cast plays. Our current one, a play about unemployment by a twenty-one year old author from Wapping is an excellent example of an appropriate piece and it is doing a GLAA supported week's tour of London. We hope in 1982/83 to much expand this work for its own virtues and to plant seeds for the main house.

We run a weekly workshop for local writers, with occasional special events for them to which GLAA contribute.

C. EDUCATION

We receive a Special Projects Grant from Newham (£12,000 in 1981/82) which is spent by us in conjunction with advice from a senior member of the Newham Drama Team. This money goes on a variety of schemes and pays for most of the following work with the theatre providing all manner of assistance.

(a) The Royal's own Saturday morning youth theatre which occasionally performs in the main house and the studio.

(b) Special school tours.

(c) Under a scheme called Actorship we send main house actors into schools to work on texts and projects as suggested by teachers.

(d) Local schools visit to stage several one-night stand productions during the year, and we co-operate closely with the Newham Youth Theatre to stage their prestige main production for a week in our theatre and to run for a four-week summer school.

(e) In association with Newham Education Department we mount the Newham International Festival of TIE which uses theatre facilities for one week a year and brings in TIE groups from all over the world.

(f) Two weekend courses for schoolteachers in 1981.

(g) We are working as full partners with Newham Arts Council to launch a new Arts Centre, a few hundred yards from the theatre and to establish a new community theatre there under a Manpower Services Commission scheme.

D. Amateur

We spend no subsidy money under this heading, indeed some events raise considerable money for our Building Fund. They are subsidized only in the sense that the existence of the building as a going concern allows them to take place, but they are an important part of our programme for local, national and theatrical goodwill.

Examples of amateur activities are hiring for conferences or shows by trade unions, local amateurs and schools. The agents and casting directors stage their annual pantomime for two nights and Transport House its annual revue.

Summary

We bring international artists to create new shows and provide entertainment on our main stage. We co-operate closely with the local education department and local schools and organizations. We have managed in 1980/81 to set our house in order financially and administratively. Our box office income, despite continuing our generous concessions to old-age pensioners, the unemployed and students, is increasing appreciably in relation to subsidy. We made it an important priority in 1981/82 to improve our marketing and will continue to do so. In 1982/83, alongside the heartening progress being made in the total refurbishment of our beautiful building, we are looking forward to continuing our bold policy on the main stage, to expanding our studio work and to investing with the help of many other sources of subsidy, time and energy working with the local community in all manner of projects. We are a highly individual local international theatre.

Of the undertakings mentioned in the report, the agent's and casting director's pantomime is the most notorious; during the last production a merry Julie Walters pointed to the stage, and shouted 'That's my fucking agent up there, dressed as a fairy'. The variety night is unique and increasingly popular and features guest and regular actors submitting themselves to a Victorian music-hall atmosphere – vociferous negative opinion included – for the sum of £20 per performance.

Kate Williams, along with Michael Elphick ('Stratford to me means East, not upon Avon'), is now a constant variety night host. She performed in her first one in 1973, in front of an audience which included Joan Littlewood. Her contribution was to run on stage, deliver a succession of quick-fire jokes, and run off again. After a fifteen-strong opera pastiche group decided to exit from the same side of the stage as Williams was supposed to enter; she found herself forcibly delayed. Then a well-known face due to the success of the television series 'Love They Neighbour', she was harshly judged by the most knowledgeable critic in the house: 'Oh, isn't that a typical telly star,' said Joan Littlewood, 'she has to wait before she makes a grand entrance.'

The production which tilted the balance in Stratford's favour came shortly after Philip Hedley's report to the Arts Council. Nell Dunn, whose grandfather was the man who broke the bank at Monte Carlo, had risen to fame as the author of *Up the Junction* and *Poor Cow,* books which provoked outrage, questions in Parliament and delight among those seeking a more authentic contemporary British fiction. Her first stage play was set in a women's Turkish bath, and was entitled *Steaming*. It reached Hedley via Knightsbridge Productions, he arranged a read-through with six actresses and immediately decided to stage it at the Theatre Royal as quickly as possible.

Nell Dunn says of it: 'For me, as it was my first stage play, the technical problems seemed impossible. I didn't know how things were meant to be, knew virtually nothing about theatre. Having a director willing to take a chance on it was success enough, I don't think anybody saw it as a transfer or an enormous

Georgina Hale played the leader of the women fighting to keep an East End steam bath open. 'For the first two previews the theatre was at best half empty; Philip rushed around telling us that it was quite normal, everything was OK. It wasn't. Then, on the third preview, we were sold out. You couldn't get a ticket after the first week, and the run at Stratford was extended.' But the success of the production cannot be ascribed to helpful reviewers. Rosalind Carne in the *Financial Times* began her piece: 'Nell Dunn's first stage play is shot through with extravagant and caustic wit. Verbal sparkle, a strong cast, at least two intriguing characters and some fine visual embellishments are promising ingredients and the opening moments bode well. But the finished piece is curiously disappointing, a package of fine trappings around a central dramatic void.

Individual performances received praise, especially those of Georgina Hale and Maria Charles, but few critics thought the play itself anything more than a noble effort. Word of mouth, fortuitous and carefully delivered publicity and the pull of the extraordinary setting of the play made up for disappointing notices. Despite part of the ceiling falling in on Brenda Blethyn, who was taken to hospital with two broken fingers, the performances of *Steaming* tended to improve as audiences became more willing to be entertained and the cast grew comfortable in the new environment. Georgina Hale found Stratford East entirely different from any other theatre she had played in.

> I'd never experienced the sight of people lighting up cigarettes and drinking pints of beer in the audience before. It was unnerving. But there was another side to that attitude: the marvellous response we had. I can remember a party of cleaners we had in — when one of the girls had to say how efficient a Pifco was, one of the cleaners stood up and shouted 'There'll be a run on 'em tomorrow!' Made it great!

Steaming went on to win awards, and transferred to the Comedy Theatre where it ran for two years. Stratford East did not have to wait that long before it produced another West End show. In April 1982 Alan Plater's *On Your Way Riley!* with Maureen Lipman and Brian Murphy attracted the attention of several London producers. Plater had wanted his work about the relationship between Kitty McShane and Arthur Lucan to be performed at Stratford, seeing it as a 'punters' theatre, one of the few'. He was, however, quite willing for a central London transfer to take place, and it was the Falklands war which damaged the play's chances. As people ignored the theatre and sat in front of the television screen, anxious to hear news of the empire's progress, angels who had previously registered interest began to disappear. Maureen Lipman was disappointed, but enjoyed the production.

> The correct venue for the correct show, in fact it might not have worked in town. Jobbing actors are the best for Stratford, stars don't quite fit in. We needed more money on the set and on publicity, but the number of good ghosts at that place always brings you through. On the first day there we were addressed by the director, then by the administrator, and then by the cleaner. No delusions of grandeur. The production succeeded because it began before the show, in the bar with songs and drink and conversation. I don't want to romanticize poverty and poor conditions, but the sense of

involvement and family at the theatre is moving, very moving. I still get letters from people who saw that show.

The next production's transfer was never in any doubt. Australian singer Robyn Archer's *A Star is Torn* consisted of portrayals of eleven female performers who had suffered both for their art and their sex. It was to move to Wyndham's in August; before then it received reviews the like of which Stratford had not seen since the most glorious days of Workshop.

The *Guardian's* Michael Billington was a thoughtful observer:

The finest of many fine things about Robyn Archer's *A Star is Torn* at the Theatre Royal, Stratford East, is that she seems more interested in her subject (the tragic destruction of so many female singers' lives) than in projecting herself.

Yet, such is the paradox of art, you come out hymning Ms Archer's own opulent talent: her seemingly effortless ability to conjure up a vast range of singers from Marie Lloyd to Janis Joplin, her capacity to deliver each phrase into your lap, her blend of celebration and lament.

Her thesis broadly is that women singers over the last century have often been wrecked by artistic schizophrenia: by the need to project female vulnerability in their songs and their lives, while at the same time displaying the autocratic charisma of the solo performer.

Hence the frequent dives into drink, drugs, marital instability (the eleven women evoked had a total of thirty-one husbands), and early death. As a thesis, it makes a lot of sense. My only niggle would be that Marie Lloyd (a born battler) fits into it a little uneasily, and that it underplays audience blood-lust: a sound I last heard at the Palladium where the audiences seemed to be willing Liza Minnelli into a state of violent emotional excess.

But what makes *A Star is Torn* riveting is that Ms Archer combines intelligent commentary with ironic evocation – in that sense, it is a classic Brechtian show. She doesn't impersonate: she presents.

Thus she moves easily from a young, gingham-frocked Judy Garland, singing 'I'm Nobody's Baby', to a gardenia-decked Billie Holiday, all honey and molasses, telling us, 'I've been consulted by Franklin D, even Gable had me to tea', but that she can't get her man started; and from Billie's 'No Regrets' she switches instantly into a black-frocked, wispy-haired guttural Piaf, memorably informing us, 'Je ne regrette rien.'

The vocal transitions are deft and stunning. But what matters is that Ms Archer allows you to enjoy the numbers while at the same time putting them into a critical perspective.

Brecht once wrote that the actor must not only sing but show a man singing; meaning that gesture must take precedence over emotional content. Ms Archer, directed by the show's co-deviser Rodney Fisher, follows that rule to perfection by wittily showing us Bessie Smith's spinning-top circular finger movements and Marie Lloyd's lascivious caressing of her corsetted curves.

The result is that what might, in lesser hands, have been an emotional wallow and a hindsight saga of despair becomes with Ms Archer both a generous tribute to authentic talent and a criticism of a system that encouraged its waste.

A Star is Torn, in fact, has all the complexity of first-rate theatre.

After the euphoria of *A Star is Torn* Michael Elphick starred in a new play called *Stiff Options.* Set in a funeral parlour in the North of England where a big city gangster is in hiding, it was popular with Stratford audiences but not so highly regarded by the critics. James Fenton's review in the *Sunday Times* reads in full: '*Stiff Options,* by John Flanagan and Andrew McCulloch, at Stratford East, is a comedy about undertakers – extremely short on jokes.'

Rumours of a transfer backed by Paul Raymond abounded, but nothing came of them. Despite frustrated hopes it was an eventful run for the cast and theatre staff. During rehearsals Elphick got trapped in a stage prop coffin, which knocked him virtually unconscious. Later in the season he used Philip Hedley's office as a temporary dressing-room; in the middle of an angry row between Elphick and a friend a packet of personal belongings and best wishes cards was torn up and thrown out of the window. The objects in question belonged not to Michael Elphick, but to Hedley.

In October, twenty-three-year-old playwright Tony Marchant's *The Lucky Ones* was performed on the main stage. With Phil Daniels in the leading role, the story covered the familiar but still fertile issues of unemployment, youth and the absurdities of day-to-day life. Marchant went on to become joint winner of *Drama* magazine's Most Promising Playwright award, and with a new play in the centenary year at Stratford his name is frequently associated with the theatre. As a son of East London his views on Stratford East and its style of theatre have developed over a period of years:

When I first began to write seriously I sent my work off to the Royal Court; they returned it, saying that it was too much like Nigel Williams. Now I'd never heard of Nigel Williams. Stratford treats people in an entirely different way, judges you in terms of personality more than in terms of literature. The comparison with the Court is inevitable; one is intimidating, the other comfortable and inviting; one in the middle of an area that few working-class young people go to, the other just the opposite. If Stratford hadn't been as supportive I for one would have probably given up writing. You can easily get depressed by the liberal voyeurism which permeates the theatre in this country, become tired of seeing people pretend to be cockneys. If there is such a thing as youth theatres, Stratford has got to figure heavily.

The 1983 season started off with a visit from Scotland's Wildcat Theatre Company with an anti-nuclear piece entitled *Any Minute Now*. Three months later Mustapha Matura's *Welcome Home Jacko* was revived. Although it lacked much of the verve of the original rendering, it played to full audiences, largely composed of black youngsters.

For *Short of Mutiny* by Daniel Mornin, the press office at Stratford decided to create its own publicity. After covering the front of the Old Vic, then dark, with posters for the show the Vic's office was inundated with telephone calls inquiring about a new play called *Short of Mutiny*. When patrons of the National Theatre and Barbican were handed leaflets advertising the Stratford show official complaints were made, but the campaign had achieved its ends.

The production's strong language and realistic depiction of life on board a Royal Navy battleship pleased and irritated reviewers in equal proportions. Philip Hedley directed the play, and managed to use a cast of over twenty with an adroitness which many in the profession found remarkable. Actor Michael Bryant was only one of the many who personally wrote to the theatre to express admiration – an act which, according to Hedley, 'certainly compensated for a poor review or two'.

In June, 7:84 Theatre Company Scotland left an indelible impression with its *Men Should Weep*. Irving Wardle wrote in *The Times*:

> When a long-neglected play from the old Unity Theatre repertory is rediscovered in the author's lifetime, revived by a director of international reputation, and swept into London on a tide of Scottish acclaim, it is hard to present it as anything other than a deserving cause.
>
> But as soon as you start dwelling on Ena Lamont Stewart's affinity with O'Casey, and saluting her study of Glaswegian tenement life in the 1930s for its humane testimony and grim relevance to modern Britain, the response is to be one of dutiful assent followed by a stampede for the exit.
>
> I do not know how *Men Should Weep* appeared to its original 1947 audiences. But its success in Giles Havergal's 7:84 company production is that it departs from all the old conventions of the Socialist stage. Here we have Maggie, worn out with her scrubbing job and looking after seven

children and an unemployed husband, but still unsoured and full of love for them all. She is a splendid, wholly credible woman; but it would be an insult to call her an heroic working-class matriarch.

Then there is the rest of the family; the runaway daughter, the disastrously married son, parasite granny, and the swaggeringly unmanned head of the household. You can like and dislike all of them in different ways; but so far as the play is concerned, they are given no alibi for their mistakes and cruelties. It is for the audience to draw the wider social lesson.

There are some fierce domestic rows and one near-fatal stabbing; but what is most remarkable about the piece is its wealth of really funny lines, and the fact that it avoids all censoriousness towards a group of characters who are incessantly judging each other.

If ever there was a claustrophobic box set around them, no trace of it survives in the free air of this production. On Geoff Rose's stage, the Morrisons occupy a ramshackle downstage area, backed by a grimy concrete skyline haunted by spying neighbours, snogging couples, and late-night rowdies; while members of the family double as a chorus of gossips and other figures from the outside.

With the exception of one small boy, age is presented entirely through acting, with the handsome young Jo Cameron Brown emitting bird-like squawks as the senile granny, clamping boneless gums on any passing sweet and clasping her pension book in palsied talons.

The aim, superbly achieved, is to dispel emotional intensity, and divert attention from these people as individuals to the conditions in which they are compelled to live. And instead of the plod of naturalistic narrative there are side-lit tableaux, explosions of brilliantly lit energy, bold groupings (as where all the women line up down-stage for cake-nibbling courtship confessions), and moments of vertical take-off into lurid violence and volcanic farce.

In short, Mr Harvergal has effected a triumphant marriage between the allegedly decadent style of the Citizen's Theatre and the wholesome virtues of the old Labour stage. Acknowledging that, the sharpest memory is of the richly eloquent Glasgow dialogue, and of Elizabeth MacLennan's gently implacable central performance.

The year finished with *Gas and Candles,* a quaint comedy about two old-age pensioners which was a catastrophe at the box office, *Pericles* staged by David Ultz, and a Christmas *Sleeping Beauty,* with boisterous child audiences wolf-whistling everybody who came on stage.

Before it was two months' into its centenary year, Stratford East incurred yet more criticism. Two black plays, *El Dorado* and *Two Can Play* did well enough but *Breakneck,* a version of the Ruth Ellis story by Vince Foxall, fared badly — Kate Williams passed out after catching her foot in some stage machinery, one actress dried on the opening night, and reviews were uniformly damning. Ken Hill's *Phantom of the Opera* restored some hope and another Barrie Keeffe production *A Mad World My Masters,* in which was depicted a striptease by the Prime Minister, appealed at least to Labour Party groups who came to the theatre *en masse.*

The theatre productions to complete 1984 were Trevor Rhone's *Old Story Time,* imported directly from Jamaica, Tony Marchant's new play *Lazy Days Limited* and for pantomime, a Stratford rendering of *Red Riding Hood.* The variety nights still attract large followings and still provide the background for outrageous performances and advertising stunts: press officer Mark Borkowski informed the media that one such evening would feature a tap-dancing dog, which had even danced on the streets of San Francisco. Then, to the horror of canine fanciers everywhere the animal was run over and killed on a pre-performance walk. The ensuing publicity was extraordinary; in fact — of course — there was never any such dog. A suitable beginning to the Theatre Royal's second hundred years.

Panto Stratford style: *Sleeping Beauty,* 1983

Modern black theatre with ambiguous results – *Two Can Play,* 1984

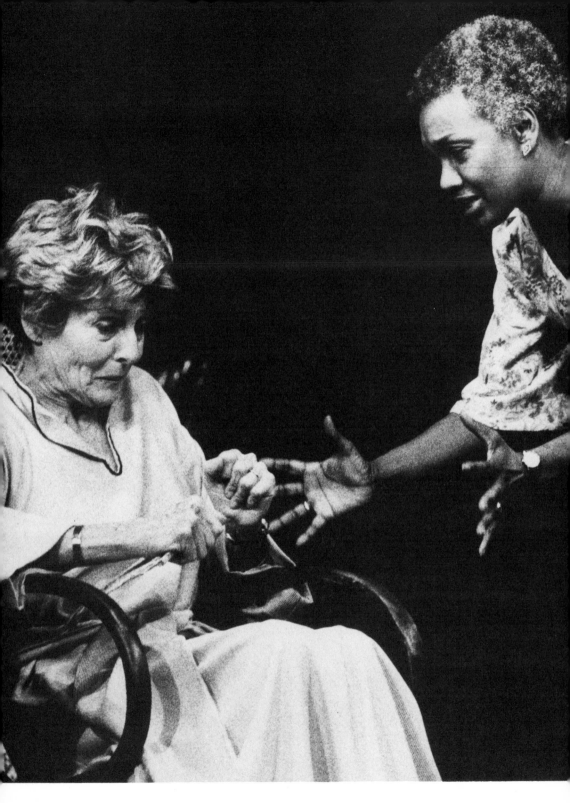

El Dorado, 1984

Loved by the public, hated by the press—*Breakneck,* 1984

Kate Williams in 1980s variety

4.
Futures

A concluding chapter often has to justify its own existence, and an author may find it difficult to do so. That is not the case with this volume. At the time of writing the Greater London Council, central in the funding of the Theatre Royal, is under severe threat from a Conservative government. The black community is in the process of finding its artistic feet, both as an audience and as performers and writers. And the theatre as a viable means of entertainment, in the face of competition from an expanding video industry is in question.

Whether the GLC survives or not lies outside the realm of this book; the effect that possible dissolution would have upon Stratford East does not. Tony Banks is a Newham member of Parliament and chairman of the GLC Arts and Recreation Committee.

> Without the GLC Stratford can look forward to a future, but to a much more uncertain one. The council has always regarded the Theatre Royal very highly because of its location, because it's one of the few theatres in outer London. It's in a solid working-class constituency, in an economically deprived part of London. It has very strong community links and roots, and it enjoys good relationships with local people. At the same time, it's far enough out to be something of a disincentive to the travelling bourgeoisie. And the quality of the productions is extremely high. So Stratford meets all the criteria of the GLC arts policy, and for that reason we've always supported it.
>
> I don't think there's very much question that Stratford is a theatre, or one of a group of theatres, which has had a very good relationship with us. That doesn't mean it's been specially privileged though. Our financial contribution is of a large dimension and frankly I can't see Newham Borough

Council, for all its enlightened attitude towards the arts, being able to replace that money if the GLC does go. I'd desperately hope that the theatre wasn't forced to close and I for one would oppose that closure in the House of Commons all the way — and I'm a pretty formidable obstacle. They'd struggle through. You see we're terribly short of resources in the East End and the Theatre Royal has a local, regional and national reputation, we can't afford to lose it.

Finally, it would probably be a point of what the theatre can continue to do, rather than one of it closing. And I must say that that's going to apply to every venue outside of the large national companies.

Arts Minister Lord Gowrie envisages no difficulty, change in approach or alteration in amount of subsidy if GLC abolition becomes a reality:

The government's attitude of course is neither here nor there. The sum allocated to individual theatres, Stratford East included, will be protected and in some cases augmented because so many borough authority bills will be taken over by the central authority, that other money will be left to be used for new purposes.

The argument that because of the political aspect of some of the Theatre Royal's work, a Conservative government would act against the theatre's interest has absolutely no foundation. The Arts Council is jealously independent, and we believe in the arm's length principle. Satire has a long tradition in this country, and this government has no intention of involving itself in censorship.

The cynical response to both men's claims would be, 'they would say that, wouldn't they?' The future financing of Stratford seems even more precarious and confusing due to the introduction of a new set of Arts Council proposals contained in their manifesto document 'Glory of the Garden'. Under this much criticized plan Stratford is one of the theatres allocated to a regional arts authority, in this case the Greater London Arts Association. The Arts Council has never been militant on behalf of the arts, and there is a well-grounded fear that being a client of a regional body will provide even less security. Philip Hedley is concerned about 'some theatres being lost in the re-shuffle' and does not trust the 'centres of excellence' approach which is the order of the day.

If GLC abolition does go ahead at some stage in the future, it is possible that the London theatres will not be farmed out, but there is no guarantee of that. Arts Council deputy drama director Jean Bullwinkle believes that some theatre managers have overreacted to the proposals: 'The relationship between the council and the companies won't be cut off, we won't lose contact. And the same criteria will be applied – quality, audience and so on. As to Stratford's budget in coming years, I can't of course say categorically whether it will change or not.' Whatever the intentions of 'Glory of the Garden', the result of it is the cutting of several small left-wing drama groups; that gives everybody at Stratford East, although they are a company with far more prestige, cause for concern.

The income and audience figures at Stratford since 1977 given in the table below reveal a mixed tale. While the number of people coming to the theatre has steadily increased, grant ratios have fallen.

YEAR	AUDIENCES	BOX OFFICE INCOME	OTHER EARNED INCOME	TOTAL EARNED INCOME	GRANT INCOME	TOTAL INCOME
77/78	33,062	£30,185	£13,061	£43,246	£119,364	£162,610
78/79	38,078	£31,147	£14,030	£45,177	£155,217	£200,394
79/80	40,681	£53,692	£26,351	£80,053	£170,115	£250,158
80/81	48,693	£75,812	£33,400	£109,212	£196,590	£305,802
81/82	52,318	£126,417	£47,492	£173,909	£242,426	£416,335
82/83	71,507	£167,091	£57,491	£224,582	£277,993	£502,575

The grant to Stratford is made up of contributions from the Greater London Council, the Arts Council, the London borough of Newham and a tiny sum from the London borough of Waltham Forest. The overall ratio of grant per pound of income has diminished as shown in the following table.

YEAR	GRANT PER £ INCOME
77/78	£2.76
78/79	£3.44
79/80	£2.13
80/81	£1.80
81/82	£1.39
82/83	£1.24

As the figures creep ominously towards the often mentioned pound for pound subsidy, Philip Hedley must have doubts, especially if a Conservative administration decides to impose its will on the arts establishment. Hedley's comment is: 'We've always functioned at our best when we're faced with a challenge. I mean that, excuse the cliché. From Joan Littlewood's time to the danger-list period this theatre has intensified efforts and improved results when there are problems. Is art and drama meant to thrive when all is comfortable and secure?'

Stratford's application for a larger grant for the coming period reveals its proposals for the future. Under the heading 'Statement of Policy', the aim is expressed:

. . . to make the theatre accessible to new theatregoers from our local community which in itself is made up of several different communities.

With this in mind we will continue our policy of staging mainly new or adapted plays which we believe have a particular 'popular' pull for some section of our local community . . .

To attract local audiences we stage new work mainly for the pragmatic reason that it attracts well-known actors and gains more publicity. We don't have a large regular audience who come to every play. We have to dig each audience out for each play, helped by star names and the newsworthiness of new plays. It would be impossible to do this job if we had to decrease our publicity or community relations budget.

On the obviously popular front we will of course be staging a pantomime, specially commissioned as usual, and continue our sold-out Sunday Variety Nights which are home productions, unlike in all other repertory theatres where they normally import Sunday night shows.

A secondary aim of our policy is the development of new writers, and giving writers opportunities on a main stage, opportunities that seem to be becoming rarer year by year in British theatre. Because it is essential, for a new play policy, to have as a wide a choice as possible we are budgetting in 1984/85 to increase the average size of cast from ten to twelve.

Our third aim, underpinning our whole policy, will continue to be community involvement through our admired and original schools service called Actorshop, through talks and theatre tours, through forays into the local community such as presenting a short play in Urdu for Asian community centres, through our youth groups and through assisting local schools and youth groups to present work on our stage.

In the second half of the document, lead by the question 'Please state to what degree the company is achieving its current aims and objectives', Hedley wrote:

In 1983/84 our most obviously 'populist' shows, the pantomime and the Variety Nights, were splendid box-office successes. So was the 7:84 visit with *Men Should Weep*. Two of our three black plays have done well at the box office. The third black play, our other two new plays and our production of *Pericles* came in below box-office targets, despite generally excellent reviews in the case of *Pericles*.

In our primary aim to make the theatre accessible to new audiences we have been notably successful in attracting local black people to the theatre for the first time. We can boast the largest black audience of any theatre in Britain in 1983/84. It is here that we have put in a very disproportionate effort compared to financial reward but our local community is twenty-seven per cent Afro-Asian and we regard wooing them as one of our highest priorities.

Overall the box office for the new plays has been disappointing and consequently we have lowered our box office expectation for 1984/85 to what we regard as a reasonable level to achieve. We have made only modest increases in our ticket prices in 1983/84. They are already about average for surburban London theatres, and our increase in pantomime prices has put them beyond the reach of some local people.

We are determinedly trying not to increase prices and above all retain our concessions for the needy which are the lowest in London theatre e.g. £1 for best seats from Monday to Thursday (except for the pantomime). It is these concessions of course which produce the marked difference between the numbers attending our theatre and our box office take. Keeping prices low is much favoured by our local authority and is an important plank in our much-increased application to the GLC . . .

Most of the coming problems, and solutions, are contained in Hedley's appeal. On one aspect especially, that of black audiences, the future of the theatre rests heavily. West Indian and Asian comunities have not yet taken to the live entertainment which is on offer in a particularly significant way; all black productions staged at major theatres are primarily for white audiences. The Theatre Royal is one of the very few mainstream, first-night review venues in the middle of an immigrant area. For Stratford East that gives rise both to opportunities and problems. The staging of two black plays in such a short space of time was seen by some as a negative approach; the appeal to black audiences, it was suggested, should have been carried out in a less direct manner.

The run of *Welcome Home Jacko,* with a cast which was very popular with young West Indians, attracted the expected audience, but alienated others. There is an undoubted racial tension in Stratford, and the spontaneity of appreciation, or lack of it, by a black audience of a play is very different from the subdued murmurs or applause of the traditional English theatregoers. *Welcome Home Jacko,* while successful, and illustrative of black theatre at its sparkling best, did not succeed with sections of the white population of East London.

With a possible all-Indian *A Midsummer Night's Dream* in the planning stages for a future season and an increasingly vocal and important Afro-Asian community in Stratford, the theatre has to tread the balance between ghetto-ization and the possible loss of a huge and artistically fertile black audience. Mustapha Matura, leading black playwright and author of *Welcome Home Jacko* states that: 'As more and more black writers come to the surface they're obviously going to be looking for venues to put on their plays. Stratford will be a certain choice, there's a scarcity of theatres for black writers. It has an important, central part in the future of black theatre'.

Hedley's emphasis on publicity as a vital strand in the theatre's future is significant. At present Mark Borkowski – known as 'King of the Diaries' – and the publicity office receive less than £5,000 per production for total expenditure. They invariably go over budget. If subsidies to Stratford East are reduced the promotions sector, despite Hedley's commitment to it, will be one of the first to suffer; that would do untold damage to the Theatre Royal's profile and destroy any structure of campaign that Borkowski has established. 'My first job was in a bacon curing factory' he says, 'and so I've gone from selling hams to selling hams. But without financial support it can't be done'.

Daily Mail critic Jack Tinker believes that the Theatre Royal is a favoured venue among his associates, but is worried about the coming years.

> Very, very pessimistic. It has twenty years of loyalty, and there is no way the products of the theatre would let it die without a fight. But with television expansion and money problems I can see a struggle to survive, and perhaps a losing one.
>
> The artistic dilemma has built up for the last ten years, and hasn't yet been solved. There's no real reason for it being there, much as one loves it. You'd be terribly upset at its going because of historical points and so on, but I do wonder how much it would be missed. There is too much complacency at Stratford, too much of a hit and miss policy. You do come away being more warmed by their good intentions than artistic merit, a bit like watching your family perform charades.

Old style entertainment

Michael Elphick. A love affair with the theatre and the area   44

A not untypical variety night act of the 1980s

In between shows

46

A classic auditorium

47

Way behind the scenes

48

Stratford East's awards. The middle one is
something of an enigma

49

The theatre bar is popular with local people who seldom venture into the rest of the building

51

The staff, 1984

Tinker's view is supported by others inside London theatre, though not all are willing to let it be known. On a local scale Stratford's disappearance would be a body blow, and the town as a living community as well as a theatregoing audience would suffer dramatically: the theatre still represents dignity and prestige for Stratford. But nationally the impact would be much less. Theatrical frontiers have not been pushed back at the Theatre Royal for some time.

Michael Billington writes: 'It's still finding its artistic feet, and has only had moderate success. What Philip Hedley has done is to keep the spirit and feeling of that building alive. In the past I've got there an hour and a half early, and enjoyed the wait. That is what a theatre should be, a friendly place; and that alone is worth preserving.'

The next three years will be some of the most difficult the Theatre Royal has faced since the dark days before the arrival of Workshop. Financial cutbacks are possible, problems with artistic policy almost certain. But a generation and more of loyalty and tradition is not easily expunged. Providing sense and goodwill continues from all concerned Stratford can still exhibit that special character and atmosphere which is epitomized by an exchange between Joan Littlewood and a member of her cast only two hours before the opening of one of the biggest successes of Theatre Workshop: Joan had decided to clean the front step of the building, the actor in question came to the front door, stepped over his director, and said quite casually 'Expecting company Joan?' She was. The theatre still is.

Index

Photo Credits

Photographs appear courtesy of Newham Library Service Local Studies Library (Nos. 1–6), Howard Goorney (Nos. 7–11), Murray Melvin (Nos. 12–14, 18, 19), Victor Spinetti (Nos. 16, 17), Theatre Royal Stratford East (Nos. 15, 20, 22, 25, 26, 28, 31, 34, 52), The *Guardian* (No. 21), Maxwell Shaw (No. 23), Clare Venables/Gerry Murray (No. 24), Frazer Ashford (Nos. 27, 33), Sean Hudson (Nos. 29, 30), David Corio (Nos. 32, 35, 38, 40, 41), Ray Abbott (Nos. 36, 43), Susie Martin (No. 37), Alex Von Koettlitz (No. 39), Surinder Puri (Nos. 42, 44, 45), Jody Boulting (Nos. 46–51).